THE UNIVERSITY AND BUSINESS

T0326781

Edited by

DOUGLAS GRANT

———

V. W. BLADEN

W. E. PHILLIPS

M. ST.A. WOODSIDE

SIR ARNOLD PLANT

STANLEY F. TEELE

University of Toronto Press

1958

PREFACE

The following essays examine several aspects of a problem which is being widely discussed: the relations between the university and business. We have become increasingly aware that those engaged in business cannot satisfactorily discharge their responsibilities either to their organizations or to society until they understand the wider significance of their activities; and this understanding can only come through education. The university has therefore to accept the responsibility of seeing that those entering business receive the training most advantageous not only to their careers but also to society itself, in which the businessman today plays such a significant part. But business in its turn must shoulder a greater share of the responsibility for supporting the university, since it derives such profit from the essential training which the university affords to its executives.

The relations between the two have not been fully explored, nor have their mutual responsibilities been clearly defined, but these essays can help towards a solution of the problem. The essays by Professor V. W. Bladen, Colonel W. E. Phillips and Dean M. St.A. Woodside reflect the opinions to be found among those responsible for the policy of one Canadian university. Their essays were not written in consultation, but they are in agreement on fundamental matters. The essays by Sir Arnold Plant and Dean Stanley F. Teele show the English and American attitudes, but they, too, are in agreement with the Canadian opinion, even allowing for all national differences.

The essays were first published in 1957 as a supplement to the July number of the *University of Toronto Quarterly*, but it was felt that as they made such a notable contribution to a problem which is bound to be debated with increasing interest for several years, they should be re-issued separately in this new, independent, form.

DOUGLAS GRANT

THE UNIVERSITY AND BUSINESS

The University and Business

V. W. Bladen
W. E. Phillips
M. St. A. Woodside
Sir Arnold Plant
Stanley F. Teele

CONTRIBUTORS

V. W. BLADEN, F.R.S.C.

Professor and Chairman of the Department of Political Economy, University of Toronto; author of *An Introduction to Political Economy*

W. E. PHILLIPS, C.B.E., D.S.O., M.C.

Chairman of the Board of Governors, University of Toronto

M. St.A. WOODSIDE

Dean of the Faculty of Arts, University of Toronto

SIR ARNOLD PLANT

Sir Ernest Cassel Professor of Commerce, University of London; author of *The Population Problem*, etc.

STANLEY F. TEELE

Dean, Graduate School of Business Administration, Harvard University

JOHN F. CHAPMAN

Associate Editor, *Harvard Business Review*

The Rôle of the University —— *V. W. Bladen*

"Men are men before
they are lawyers or physicians or manufacturers; and if you make them
capable and sensible men, they will make themselves capable and sensible lawyers or physicians." This statement of John Stuart Mill, which
might have ended with a reference to manufacturers or businessmen,
ought to be carefully considered by university administrators and by
business leaders. In these days of pressure for education *in* business
administration, it is well to consider whether the university in performing
its ancient function of liberal education may not in fact provide a better
education *for* business than can be provided by some of the newfangled
courses in Business Administration. I shall argue that modern business
needs to recruit educated men and should not worry about what they
are educated in. But while business needs educated men it also needs
trained men: some of this training is properly the function of the
technical institutes (e.g., Ryerson), or of the business itself; but some of
it is properly undertaken in the university. This I shall argue should be
more "education" than "training" if it is to justify a place in the university alongside the other and older professional faculties. I believe
such education should be undertaken with mature students in the
Graduate School, or in special "development" courses for experienced
executives on the model of the "staff colleges" of the armed services.

While arguing in general I am, of course, presenting a justification
of the policy of the University of Toronto in maintaining the liberal arts
character of its Commerce course and in developing a professional
course in Business Administration in the Graduate School. I shall not
claim that our Commerce course could not be better (we are always
seeking to improve it), but I do argue that it should not become less
liberal and more professional. I shall not claim that the graduate course
in Business Administration could not be improved: the University
recognized this part of its responsibility too late (1938), made much
too little provision for its work in the first twelve years after its estab-

lishment, and has not yet made adequate provision. But the principles upon which it operates are, I believe, sound; the concern continues to be with education for, rather than training in, business.

Men are men before they are businessmen; and even if it did not contribute directly to improved business management, university education would be of infinite value. For what the university seeks (or should seek) to provide is a stimulating environment in which the potentiality for growth of those who come to it can be most fully realized. It must be recognized that an environment of scholarly endeavour and research is not one in which everyone can grow best; indeed it may inhibit growth in some. It is of very great importance, therefore, to devise means of selecting those who are most likely to grow in the university and to ensure for them an opportunity to attend; it is also of great importance that alternative opportunities for growth should be provided for those for whom the university is inappropriate. It is to be deplored if social pressure, and particularly the routine requirement of a university degree for the better jobs in business, tends to push too many of the wrong students into the university: they would grow better outside and their presence in the university may well interfere with the well-being of those who can grow there. Let us all recognize, and not least the recruiting officers of business firms, that what we want are mature individuals, who have developed not only their intellectual capacity but also their imagination and their sense of values, rather than individuals who happen to have acquired a university degree and who may or may not have acquired in the process a university education. Let us not stunt the growth of any individual; but let us not assume that all individuals grow equally and in the same direction. Let us recognize, too, the danger of warping when we strive to stimulate; and let us, the teachers, be thankful that the force of growth in those students who can grow in a university is so great that warping is difficult.

This is not the place to develop a well-rounded philosophy of education, nor am I the person to do it, but something more should be said about the university before I turn to business. First let me emphasize the importance and value of the specialized honour courses which are the glory of the University of Toronto, as of many other Canadian universities. The value of these courses is that they provide the environment for growth, not that they make specialists; the honour course in Classics, it is argued, is not just for the man who wants to teach in later life, but equally for the man who may want to be a banker or an industrial relations manager. The case for the "general education" value of the specialized course has been put most effectively by Professor A. S. P. Woodhouse in *University College, 1853–1953*, and I cannot resist the opportunity to quote it and to give his words wider currency.

Here, then, is a striking example of the way in which University College, through the work and influence of Hutton, gave direction to the aims and methods of the Arts course at the honour level. For honour Classics, as we have observed, furnished a model and set the pace for other honour courses in the Humanities. The special marks of these honour courses at Toronto are: the selection of a sufficiently important and productive area of concentration—the Classics, it may be, or the ancient Semitic world, or English, or two of the other languages of modern Europe—an area with its own internal relations and its recognizable contribution to life today; the systematic exploration of this area as supplying the principal content and the focus of a four-year course; the insistence on the command of texts as the basis of the whole effort—the reading of the books themselves, not the acquisition of mere information about them; the generous conception of literature, which extends beyond *belles-lettres* to include the literature of ideas, but studied always as literature addressed to the general reader; the placing of these texts in their historical setting, with the result of illuminating the texts and of gradually giving to the student such command of the history of his area as no series of survey courses ever achieved, and finally as the outcome of it all, possession not only of a considerable body of the world's best knowledge, but of a habit of mind and a point of view which might also be a starting point for further exploration. Classics was the first course effectively to demonstrate in Canada the grand aim of the honour system, general education by means of judicious specialization. But the description attempted above will apply, *mutatis mutandis*, to all the rest.

Let the student coming to the university choose the course in which he is most likely to grow—the course which is most likely to excite and stimulate him. At that stage he should not be asking if this course will train him for a profession, or whether the recruiting officers of business will pay any serious attention to graduates of it.

This belief that the specialized honour course has value in providing general education and that the object of university education is to promote growth rather than the acquisition of knowledge, leads to some views about the character of university teaching. Nowhere have I seen these better stated than in an unpublished memorandum by Professor Pigou. I hope I shall be forgiven for quoting a part of it. Professor Pigou was protesting against the views of some teachers of economics of "their young men as a set of sausage skins, to be appropriately stuffed, with the ends neatly tied up in preparation for the grand assize of the Tripos! The meat, to be really satisfactory, must contain the very latest facts, and, for Part II, the very latest bits of theoretical apparatus. . . . The young men are to be taught economics; told that this question possesses that answer." This he admitted was an exaggeration, even a caricature, but it provided a foil for his thesis. "According to my notions," he said, "undergraduates ought not to be regarded as sausage skins. They are human beings to be educated, or better still, to be allowed to educate themselves. . . . Having failed myself to 'master' Economics in 40 years I am less optimistic than some of my colleagues that ordinary undergraduates can master it in one year or even in three. But they *can* be interested and stimulated and helped to some growth of mind. . . . I would never 'teach' them Economics. Marshall did not 'teach' us: he talked to us in an interesting way about interesting things, and, by that means, developed in us some rudiments of intelligence. . . . What these young men need is cooperation, not spoon-feeding: the University touch, not the crammers'." This memorandum I re-read yearly in the hope that I can attain the "University touch," in spite of my own failings and the fact that I am responsible for hundreds of students rather than the tens that the claims of real education would dictate.

This is no new doctrine, that a really liberal education is not only valuable in the development of men as whole men, but in preparation for their development as businessmen; Sir Daniel Wilson preached it before the Legislature of the Province of Ontario in 1890. "I am persuaded," he said, "that no training is better qualified to fit men for many practical duties than the persistent diligence of systematized study in any of the departments of university Honour work. . . . Our aim in the Faculty of Arts is high culture in its truest sense, the pursuit of knowledge for its own sake, and wholly independent of mere professional requirements. But if a result of such training is to secure able and scholarly teachers for our schools, for our bankers men of clearer insight into the principles on which the wealth of nations depend, for lawyers and judges men of cultivated intellect trained in wide fields of philosophic speculation . . . and for physicians men who have advanced beyond the stage of clinical instruction and as scientific experts can render a reason for the courses they pursue; surely this is a public gain." And Stephen Leacock many years ago addressing a meeting of businessmen in Montreal said: "Education is a peculiar process. You aim at one thing and you hit another. You set out to look for ultimate truth and you don't find it but incidentally you have acquired a cultivated mind. You pursue studies that you think will be of use in your business. They are not. But by the time you are done with them you yourself are a better man for your business or for any other business. . . . If you pursue your studies with too directly practical an aim you miss the mark. The worst influence that bears on our present day education is the exaggerated demand that it should be practical. It ought only to be practical by accident." And well do I remember Professor C. R. Fay in the early twenties reporting to a group of Toronto businessmen that Anglo-Persian Oil had recruited the winner of the prize for Greek verse at Cambridge as a result of their search for men of "high saturation value," men who could quickly learn the business and develop executive talent. Finally I find my colleague Professor Ashley in a memorandum to Dr. Cody in 1937 arguing against the professionalization of our Commerce and Finance course: its object, he said, is "to turn out graduates who can expect to apply themselves with success to the task of learning a business quickly, of becoming good citizens, and of living a full life."

Though I direct the attention of the recruiting officer for business to the writer of Greek verse, or the graduate in Philosophy, I do not intend in any way to distract his attention from our graduates in Commerce and Finance. They too have a liberal education, primarily in economics and economic history; they are more likely to be seeking a business career; and we are not quite so pure and consistent that some "practical" studies have not crept in. It is a tribute to business and its recruiting officers that the inclusion of such practical subjects in a man's programme does not increase the demand for him. Their inclusion does sometimes help a student to find himself; and in the atmosphere of the honour course these practical subjects tend to become philosophical, educational.

II

Let me turn for a moment to business. There has been evident for some years an increasing interest on the part of business in university education, an increasing recognition of its value, an increasing demand for university graduates. This has not been entirely because of the need for more and more highly trained scientists: the problem of the training, or rather education, of pure and practical scientists, is of vital importance to us all, but it is a problem which I am not competent to discuss. I confine myself to the increasing demand for university graduates for "management," or "administration." I should like to discuss briefly why, in my opinion, this demand for graduates in the liberal arts (including Commerce and Finance) should increase, why business should be interested in supporting this essential core of higher education. I shall not attempt to estimate why the demand has increased, or to determine how far business has been motivated by the three reasons I propose to give. (The first is probably the most important explanation of this increase, but I am conscious of a growing awareness of the second and third reasons, though there may be very different ways of expressing them.) First, the increasing difficulty of business management, resulting from size, complexity, and technological and social change, has made it more and more necessary to acquire for each corporation and for business as a whole an adequate and increasing share of the very limited supply of potential administrative talent, of the potential leaders. Second, the new status of business leaders in an industrial or "business" civilization imposes obligations of social leadership which involve an understanding not only of business but of society too. Third (a corollary of the second), the new status of business leaders imposes on them an obligation to represent the "values" of our society, moral and aesthetic. These last two reasons, of course, derive from the fact that businessmen have become the new aristocracy and they must learn—as indeed many have learnt—that *noblesse oblige*, whether the *noblesse* is conferred by the sovereign or earned by business achievement.

But it is also becoming clear that these qualities, intellectual and moral, are needed for the solution of what I believe to be the most serious problem of business administration in the next generation—the problem of securing real co-operation on the part of most of those involved in the economic process. Again I am out of my depth, having available only a paragraph in which to develop a point requiring a book and a more competent author. But I believe that a solution of this problem is vital not only to our success in production but to the viability of our civilization. If by my words I can interest even a few people in the search for understanding of these problems, and particularly if I can interest a few scholars and businessmen in working together on these problems, I shall feel that my effort has been amply rewarded. And if this point of view is accepted it has important implications for part III of this paper, in which I shall return to the university and its work in business administration.

Perhaps what I should do is simply to say—read Elton Mayo's books, *Human Problems of an Industrial Civilization* and *Social Problems of an Industrial Civilization*. They do not contain the solution to these problems, but they are, I believe, most persuasive; and after reading them one is more likely to be asking the right questions. But let me raise five points to explain my interest in stimulating the interest of business-men in these problems of "human relations in administration."

First, as an economist, I am concerned with the increase of wealth and conscious of how far we are from an "economy of plenty." Of immediate interest is the productivity necessary to sustain our defence effort, to meet our increased demand for leisure, and yet to improve the standard of living of the vast majority of the people. Can we in such circumstances neglect the possibility of increased production through improved co-operation? Professor E. H. Phelps Brown put it this way in his inaugural address at London University:

Let me now consider how this growing insight into human nature affects our view of the prospects of labour. A point of great practical importance presents itself immediately. There is a reason to believe that our national product can to-day be substantially increased, without installing any more equipment, if men who are now working only reluctantly and listlessly, who "couldn't care less," could come to work willingly and with interest. The possibility of such an increase is not a matter of conjecture, but is established by known differences between the results obtained by different firms in the same trade or by the same group of workers at different times. The increase does not come from speeding up, nor even from the worker being willing to put more effort into the job. It comes about without increased exertion, through the liberation of human energies that occurs when inner conflicts are resolved and social frustrations are removed. When interest succeeds boredom, and pride in achievement takes the place of indifference, when we work with a common purpose instead of at cross purposes, then we can get more done in a day without being any more tired at the end of it.

In these days of "full employment" we have no more "manpower" but we have not used up our reserve of "willpower."

Second, we have relied too much, in the past, on pecuniary incentives and the fear of unemployment. Now it is clear that fear never did succeed in releasing the potential of human achievement; at best it guaranteed a certain minimum performance. But even if fear were more effective than I suggest we have surely to rule it out. On the lowest level one can say that its use is no longer politically feasible (the politically tolerable level of unemployment is now very low, perhaps too low for adequate flexibility and mobility). On a higher level, such a solution is in conflict with the values of liberal democracy, of the way of life we claim to be defending. If we dismiss "fear" can we likewise dismiss pecuniary incentives? This is a more difficult question, but I have argued elsewhere that you cannot "buy co-operation." This is not to rule out the effectiveness of pecuniary incentives in general but to argue that they are only effective in a "good society." Professor T. N. Whitehead put the same point in his *Leadership in a Free Society*: "A wage system designed to evoke high motivation is apt to increase the force of the motives already in being. If they are favourable to the policies of management well and good; but if they be otherwise, the more the employees are motivated the more they will resist their nominal leaders." Or again: "If the group is reacting against the purposes of its management, then it is likely that the added incentives may be taken as one more proof of management's attempt to drive its workers."

Third, the difficulty of management in securing co-operation is made much greater by the speed of technological change. Everyone fears change. To tap the reserve of willpower in face of this fear of, and resistance to, change, and to secure the tremendous productive (and defence) advantages of this rapid development of technology, constitutes one of the greatest problems for, and challenges to, the business leaders of the future. Social scientists have learnt something about this problem, but not nearly enough; and some businessmen have applied some of this knowledge, but only too few.

Fourth, as an economist of the old school I am concerned not only with production but also with "real cost," the wear and tear of human tissue, and not least of nervous tissue: and as a citizen I am worried about what production does to men. Again let me quote Professor Phelps Brown:

With all our present problems, there is little left of the poverty which was systematic and endemic forty years ago. What then is the way forward now? To yet higher levels of real income, from the European to the American factory-worker's standard of consumption, and on again beyond that? perhaps so; yet what are refrigerators and radios and cars, if they come with more personal instability, more broken homes, more insecure and inwardly-tormented children? Even to-day, which causes more suffering among wage-earners, lack of the things which can be bought, or the anxieties, frustrations, and conflicts of neurosis?

I would add that there is a positive aspect as well as a negative one: there is the possibility of an "income" of satisfaction from doing the work itself.

Finally, I suggest that a new problem for management arises from the progressive achievement of political and social democracy. This is not to suggest that "authority" is unnecessary: it is to suggest that "authoritarianism" (an insistence on authority for its own sake, an arbitrary authority or, as Mary Parker Follett put it, an insistence on the authority of "mere position" rather than of "function") is dangerous. It is to suggest that leaders have to earn real authority and cannot have it conferred upon them from above.

I end this section with a quotation from Professor O. H. Taylor's book *Economics and Liberalism*, a book which I have been commending to many of my friends in business for its fine statement of the values which I believe to be implicit in their adherence to free enterprise:

"I cannot believe that—within this country or any of the relatively prosperous truly liberal capitalist countries—the main causes of wide prevalence and high intensities of extreme oppositional or obstructive attitudes threatening and hampering liberal capitalism lie at all in its economic imperfections. . . . For all its faults, liberal capitalism or the system of free enterprise, wherever it really exists and has a chance to function, is on the whole unmistakably a very excellent economic system with respect to its service to the economic welfare of the people generally—by far the best in this respect that the world has ever known or knows today. . . . It is not in the economic respect but in other respects, primarily, that our capitalist economic and general society as it is, but need not remain with no modifications, has traits and a mode of operation tending to engender widespread emotional attitudes and views and forms of behavior inimical to it. . . . My suggestion is that there lies behind all this something else beyond or beneath peoples' economic interests. . . . The fundamental causes lie, I suspect, in excessive frustrations of peoples' non-economic and non-rational but inevitable natural, human, and legitimate emotional needs; for sufficient, tolerable degrees of relative stability, continuity, and security, not of their incomes alone but of their local, personal, family, and group and community ways of life. . . . Frustration of emotional needs of this sort produces a dim sense of living in an ugly, greedy, quarrelsome, hostile world; and the hatred produced by fear is directed at capitalism, the competitive system, big business."

If this is a sound diagnosis, and I believe it to be sound enough to take very seriously, the future of liberal society depends very much on the success of businessmen (amongst whom I include trade-union leaders) in finding ways of making efficient production consistent with the "good life." Political change may help, but almost certainly cannot solve the problem. Indeed it is possible that the viability of even the Soviet system is dependent on a solution of this administrative problem! In the search for solutions economists and teachers and practitioners of business administration must collaborate with anthropologists (particularly the new "applied" variety), sociologists, social psychologists, and psychiatrists in order to learn, in Professor Taylor's words, "what conditions of life are required for tolerable emotional health and contentment or serenity, and how prevailing practices in free economic society might better provide and permit such conditions without undue interference with economic requirements."

III

It remains to consider the relevance of all this to the rôle of the university in education in business administration, to the rôle in this University of its Institute of Business Administration. A few general propositions seem to follow from what has been said so far. First, the Institute should insist that its function is education, not training. It should therefore resist the pressure of special groups to provide specific training for particular jobs. The object of university work in industrial relations, for example, is to turn out men "suitable to become" rather than "made" industrial relations officers. They may be less useful immediately than better trained and less well-educated men, but I believe that they will be more useful ultimately. Specific training for the job must be done on the job. Indeed, not only the training, but the education of the next generation of managers is a vital function of the managers of this generation. The university can help. But it cannot perform this task. Nor can a staff training department. Education of his subordinates should be recognized as a vital function of the executive; the master-apprentice relationship has to be established in management; the "coaching" of the junior by his senior is the surest source of education and executive development.

More important than the problem of what to teach is the problem of how to teach. The staff in any university department or school of business administration should ponder Professor Pigou's memorandum. They should not "teach" business administration; they must retain the "University touch"; their job is to help students to educate themselves, to help them to grow. This is not easy. Nor is it easy to estimate success in achieving education. But I am confident that the staff in Business Administration in this University accept this as their end, strive earnestly to achieve it, and do largely achieve it. Like their colleagues in other departments they are not satisfied with their achievement and are constantly seeking to do a better job of education.

Perhaps the selection of the teachers is more important than anything else; perhaps the real question is not what should be taught, or how it should be taught, but by whom the teaching should be done. Selection is not easy, and proof that selection has been good is even more difficult to find. We need humane men, men with a basic education in some of the social sciences, men ready to get out into the firing line occasionally as consultants, but also ready to devote a fair proportion of time and energy to independent research of a fundamental character. I emphasize here research not in terms of the responsibility of the university to contribute to the extension of the boundaries of knowledge (though I recognize such responsibility) but in terms of the necessity for continuous activity in research as a condition for effective university "teaching." Without continuous research and scholarly activity the university teacher begins to "teach" his subject; the "University touch" is lost. But all the research that should be undertaken, and, above all, the research in human problems of administration which, I have argued, is so urgent, cannot be undertaken as a by-product of teaching: funds are required to provide from time to time partial or complete freedom from teaching duties for a year or so in order that members of the teaching staff may undertake bigger research projects than are compatible with a normal teaching load, and to provide research associates capable of directing their own research and research assistants to work under direction. The programme of research in "human relations" initiated ten years ago by the Institute of Industrial Relations, and continued by the Institute of Business Administration in co-operation with the Department of Psychiatry, has petered out. Its revival is, I consider, urgent. This does not mean I think that the old programme was perfect and merely needs to be revived; it needs new tough thinking. But I am confident that there are good men anxious to do that thinking and to undertake that research when funds become available and an academic "entrepreneur" appears or is found.

The programme of evening classes for part-time candidates for the degree of Master of Commerce calls for some special comment. It is in my opinion of very great value, and of my part in its initiation I am inordinately proud, though I recognize that it is a cause of many raised academic eyebrows. I can testify that it is a very stimulating experience to conduct a class in business administration with mature students who have what Mayo called "knowledge of acquaintance" of, or experience in, the area under discussion. True, the students arrive tired; true, they miss the other elements in university life. But they are graduates who have enjoyed these other things, they are mature, they are highly motivated. Provision of these classes has been of real service to these men, to their companies, to the community: and their presence has contributed to the life of the Institute and thereby to the quality of the work done with full-time students by day. There is only one qualification to make: the numbers enrolled on this part-time basis have put a severe strain on a staff limited in size, and some of the potential good that could have been done has been lost because of this undue pressure on the staff.

What has been said of the value of evening work for the degree can be repeated with reference to the various programmes for executive development. Their value to the community and to the University is great, and the danger of neutralizing the stimulating effects on the staff by over-extension is also great. In my third Annual Report as Director of the Institute of Industrial Relations (1949) I discussed this problem and I feel that what I then said is still relevant:

> Out of our experience of the last three years I have developed a profound belief that the University has a responsibility to provide some help to mature and experienced executives both business and union. In part this means providing advanced extra-mural instruction in subjects taught at the University which have become relevant to the developing duties of the executive. More important, however, I believe, is the creation by the University staff of an opportunity for such people to think about their problems in company with others having similar problems in an atmosphere conducive to free exploration and frank exchange of experience and viewpoint.

I went on to urge the importance in such executive development programmes of attention to "human relations." This I still believe to be of prime importance, but I should now like the University to explore the possibilities of an indirect approach through a return to a study of the humanities rather than through "case" studies in the various fields of business management, finance, marketing, production, human relations, etc. My confidence in the first part of this paper is increased when I learn about the new programmes of humane studies for senior executives of some imaginative companies in the United States in collaboration with some equally imaginative universities.

Let me conclude with a quotation from Dean David of the Harvard Graduate School of Business Administration, experienced in business and education. His consideration of the qualities required for business leadership is highly relevant to the discussion of the proper education of such leaders: it certainly reinforces the plea for education rather than training for business.

In my observation, those businessmen who have been most effective in public affairs—those who, in a word, have been true business leaders in this complex world—all share certain attitudes and characteristics in addition to competence. First and foremost, these men exhibit what I like to call "tough-minded humility." The tough-mindedness is essential to competent handling of these complex problems and flows from that training and experience in calculated risk taking and decisive judgment which I have stressed. But the humility is of equal importance. It flows from a recognition of the complexities of the problems and the fact that many diverse backgrounds and talents must be brought to bear upon their solution. I am convinced that the public over a period of time does not respond to an intolerant, dogmatic, imperious, or cocky leadership in politics, in labor, or in business.

Another aspect of this tough-minded humility is the ability to respond intelligently to criticism. . . . The natural human reaction to such criticism is to be defensive, resentful, and unfortunately many a businessman—just like his critics—personalizes what are in fact great social forces. . . . The most effective business leaders I know have developed a self-restraint to handle such criticism in a positive fashion and are able to recognize constructive and justifiable criticism and to profit from it. Intelligent response to both fair and unfair criticism is essential.

Finally, there are certain characteristics which perhaps should be so obvious as not to require mention. I do mention them, however, because of some of my own recent experiences. Some of you may know that for some time I have been expounding on behalf of the Harvard Business School the doctrine of business responsibility. In trying to see what was involved I have talked with many, many people to find out what they thought. Not infrequently the words "integrity," "sincerity," and "courage" have emerged as central concepts. It goes without saying that these qualities are basic essentials. But too often we forget those things which can "go without saying." And I have reiterated the need for such qualities because of the deep concern, almost a ferment, in the minds of many—especially businessmen themselves—regarding the moral and ethical foundations of our industrial civilization.

In the war of ideas, the democracies can well use the special skills and experience which the competent businessman has so well developed in managing his own affairs. Given the other characteristics I have mentioned—and I should like, once again, to stress the attitude of tough-minded humility—the "competent businessman" can become "the responsible business leader." And I am convinced, such a responsible business leader will play a major role in helping to guide our civilization through this uncertain peace.

From the
Board Room Window

W. E. Phillips

When Winston Churchill said: "The University is a place where the future of the nation is at stake," he stated a little-recognized truth that should serve as our slogan in these challenging days. At the University of Toronto we have been conscious for several years of approaching problems which, if not resolved in time, might determine the usefulness of the University. If, in Churchill's phrase, the future of the nation is here at stake, the importance of those problems is evident. There is no mystery about their general nature. They are common to all the universities of the Western world. No two universities, however, are exactly alike, and each requires the measures appropriate to the local situation.

There are at least two specific issues which give rise to our general concern about the future. First, greatly increased numbers of young people will be seeking admission to all Canadian universities. The statistical inevitability of this conclusion is now widely accepted. The conclusion is based on the well-known studies of Dr. E. F. Sheffield of the Dominion Bureau of Statistics, in which he took into account the birth-rate figures combined with the trend towards an annual increase in the proportion of the college age group who will, in the future, seek admission to the universities. The population studies suggest that the total student enrolment in Canadian universities will rise from 71,000 in 1955–6 to 83,000 in 1960–1, and to 128,000 in 1965–6. Putting it in general terms, the student population in Canadian universities will be approximately doubled by 1965–6.

In the case of the University of Toronto, Professor B. A. Griffith has made a forecast of the student population we may expect. He projects a possible enrolment of from 14,000 to 17,000 in 1960–1, and from 18,000 to 26,000 in 1965–6. We have had experience in dealing with greatly increased numbers. Ten years ago the enrolment in Canadian universities reached a record total of 83,150, of whom 19.3 per cent were enrolled in the University of Toronto. We are not now, however, confronted by any temporary bulge in the student population, as was the case in 1947. The statisticians predict that, with rapidly increasing numbers in this part of Canada, the proportion attending the University of Toronto will rise. Certainly it is obvious that Toronto must shoulder a large share of the projected Canadian increase.

The second specific issue confronting us is the growing demand for substantially increased numbers of university graduates, particularly those with scientific and technical training.

That there is a serious shortage of scientifically and technically trained manpower in Canada is now generally recognized. That this constitutes a potential danger to national prosperity is agreed. What is not so widely understood, however, is that this problem is much more than a mere question of numbers. As Dr. J. R. Killian, the President of Massachusetts Institute of Technology, recently put it so well: "The nature of the present dearth of scientists and engineers is not simply a shortage of men. Firstly, it is a shortage of intellectual talent adequately educated in the right place. Secondly, it is more a shortage of specific talents and skills adaptable to specific areas than a general shortage of numbers."

The broad recognition of these problems has awakened a new and lively interest in the universities—"where the future of the nation is at stake." It has led to a widespread desire on the part of industry and the public generally to assist the universities in finding practical solutions.

Robert M. Hutchins has pointed out that education is a practical matter. The final results of any educational system depend upon what you want and what you can do. What you want depends upon finding an acceptable philosophy of education, and what you can do depends upon your circumstances—that is, in most cases, upon the financial support you can obtain.

As I read the history of the University of Toronto, its continued growth from the beginning has depended upon the ability of those responsible for its governance to resolve the frequent crises which, from time to time, appeared to threaten its very existence. Those crises, some of which might seem trivial today, arose with embarrassing frequency, and their resolution seems to me to have involved in each case a reappraisal of the fundamental purpose of the University in relation to the conditions then existing. If we are to avoid the temptation to find easy *ad hoc* solutions to some of our more pressing problems, we must, I am convinced, clarify in our minds the over-all fundamental objectives

of the University. We must re-state and re-affirm the purpose to which
this University is dedicated, and, having done that, seek detailed solutions to our problems within the limits of the definition of such purpose,
and, obviously, within our financial circumstances.

*

Few will dispute the fact that the role of the university has radically
changed since the day that Henry VIII felt entitled to submit the
question of the validity of his marriage to Catherine of Aragon to all
the great universities of Europe, including Oxford and Cambridge,
some of which, wise perhaps in their own generation, gave an interpretation favourable to the interests of that monstrous monarch.

During the past twenty years there has been literally a ferment of
thinking, talking, and writing about universities, their strengths and their
weaknesses, their rôle in, and their responsibility to, the communities
in which they exist and the societies they have helped to shape. Sir
Richard Livingstone, Alfred North Whitehead, "Bruce Truscot," Sir
Walter Moberly, Robert M. Hutchins, Arthur Bestor, and Hilda Neatby
have all discussed, under various titles, "the crisis in the university."
But, using "crisis" in the sense of a turning point, the greatest crisis in
higher education occurred in the nineteenth century.

Before the changes caused by the Industrial Revolution in England
were fully effective, the ancient universities were largely dominated by
the idea enunciated by John Henry Newman in 1852—the idea of an
aristocratic community of scholars eager in the pursuit of truth, perhaps
more concerned with the accumulation of knowledge than its dissemina-
tion. Newman's voice was that of the great conservative forces within
the universities that intuitively resisted change. He might be said to
represent a backward-looking concept of the university. On the other
hand, to Thomas Henry Huxley, perhaps more than to any other
individual, we owe the idea of the modern university as we now understand it.

Huxley was a vigorous and effective advocate of a more democratic
concept of the university. Fully recognizing the historic traditions of
the universities and the value of their essential spirit, he was deeply
conscious of the changes demanded by a changing society. He recognized
the ancient supremacy of the Faculty of Arts as the coping stone to the
education of the citizen, but he sought a more thorough development
of scientific and professional education.

In his rectorial address at Aberdeen in 1874, Huxley spoke of his ideal of all universities,

which, as I conceive, should be places in which thought is free from all fetters; and in which all sources of knowledge, and all aids to learning, should be accessible to all comers, without distinction of creed or country, riches or poverty. . . .

In an ideal University, as I conceive it, a man should be able to obtain instruction in all forms of knowledge, and discipline in the use of all the methods by which knowledge is obtained. In such a University, the force of living example should fire the student with a noble ambition to emulate the learning of learned men, and to follow in the footsteps of the explorers of new fields of knowledge. And the very air he breathes should be charged with that enthusiasm for truth, that fanaticism of veracity, which is a greater possession than much learning; a nobler gift than the power of increasing knowledge; by so much greater and nobler than these, as the moral nature of man is greater than the intellectual; for veracity is the heart of morality.

This is a clear statement of the trust of which we are stewards, the ideal to which we must remain true.

Let us say, then, that the purpose of the university is to provide every facility for launching young minds on a voyage of independent and creative thought. The practical problem, of course, is how to accomplish this purpose. If we agree with Hutchins' conclusions as expressed in his Marfleet Lectures delivered here in 1952, the major misfortunes in the American educational system may be traced to the enormous growth in technical schooling, free from any serious discipline of the liberal arts, or, as he puts it, "schooling without education." We are fortunate in that, historically, the University of Toronto developed from King's College as a veritable fortress of the Arts, and has emerged, after long struggles, as one of the great guardians of the traditional disciplines of the liberal arts in Canada. In the main, our professional schools— certainly the Engineering school—were born of popular demand or necessity. In their earlier stages at least, they grew up under the influence of the intimate physical contacts with the brilliant individuals who were shaping the Arts Colleges. This influence has waxed and waned, and at times has been difficult to trace. In the time of Loudon and Galbraith—two leaders who served their own times and the University well—I know that a student could spend three years in the Faculty of Applied Science and Engineering and still be blissfully ignorant of the true liberal aims of the University. Yet over the years the Faculty of Arts has infused a spirit and maintained a standard of excellence which have profoundly affected the professional schools, and we have just cause to be proud of them.

Now we must expand them, the Engineering school in particular, if we are to discharge our responsibility to community and nation. Already we are three years too late; we have been compelled to restrict admission in several faculties for the coming year, and that is unfortunate in view of the shortages that I have already mentioned. If we followed the popular demand, we would devote at once a large part of our available funds to the creation of new Engineering buildings and the addition of more Engineering staff. To many, this would appear to be the proper course of action; and, indeed, it is obvious that if we are to produce more Engineering graduates we must expand the facilities for teaching them in many ways. But "excellence" must be the constant standard of Engineering and of all other professional schools, and that standard must be set by the academic conscience of the whole University, not by one school alone, and certainly not by any outside accrediting agency or pressure group.

There is a widespread feeling that specialists cannot be well educated, that the nature of their training prevents them from being intellectually curious, imaginative, and interested in the work of others. This view is untenable: nearly all well-educated persons are, in the last analysis, specialists. Specialism so narrow as to exclude all interest in other disciplines is no preparation for democratic citizenship. In seeking the highly desirable goal of better qualified professional graduates, we must not forget that the scientific and technical field, vital though it be if we are to maintain our own industrial growth, is yet but one field of human activity.

Current discussions on the subject of the better educated engineer or technologist often end at cross-purposes, chiefly because of the failure to agree on a precise definition of the terms involved. (If I mention engineers repeatedly, it is not because they have any exclusive or preponderant importance. The same could be said of other professional graduates. But the shortage of Engineering graduates has the chief place in the public mind at the moment.) In the United Kingdom, three terms are usually employed: engineer, technologist, and technician. A recent White Paper on technical education defines a technician as one who is qualified to work under the general direction of a technologist. The technologist, however, is qualified for membership in a professional institution, and he is able to initiate practical developments in industry and to push forward the boundaries of knowledge. The engineer, we are left to assume, is a better educated technologist who has graduated from one of the established universities.

These definitions would be largely meaningless to us in Canada. We might well, however, give currency and status to the term "technologist" for those trained in institutes of technology, which are much needed and will no doubt be established in greater numbers. In the United Kingdom eight colleges of advanced technology have already been established, involving very large financial contributions by the government. There is still, I gather, a subtle distinction between the graduate from a British university and the graduate from a technological college, even as the engineer from one of the older universities is still a different type of individual from the graduate of one of the "red brick" universities. In each case the difference seems to be that one is better educated than the other.

Following the meeting of atomic scientists at Geneva a few years ago, we were permitted an insight into the startling progress the Russians were making in the training of large numbers of scientists, engineers, and technologists. We are frequently reminded of the superior scale upon which their programme is established, and it would be unwise to assume that the quality of their graduates is not good. Nevertheless there is evidence that the Russians are producing specialists in the narrow sense, force-feeding them with technology to the neglect of the arts. Moreover, the efficiency of their methods rests on a denial of individual freedom of choice. Here, committed as we are to the philosophy that education is for everyone, it still remains true that education is for the individual, and in our free society, as yet, the state does not own the individual. We must steadfastly safeguard the right of the individual to obtain the education he desires, provided that he is capable of absorbing it; and we must ensure that, as far as the universities are concerned, our professional graduates are educated for freedom—well educated.

To be well educated means different things to different people. I am certain that it must involve, as a minimum, knowledge of our language, of literature, of philosophy, of history, and, above all, some sense of moral and spiritual values.

Whether we like it or not, we are living here in an industrial society, and if our physical security alone is to be preserved, our industrial society will inevitably increase in its extent and complexity, will inevitably govern our thinking and actions for a long time to come. Surely there are few who can see in this prospect alone a salvation for our troubled world. Any reasoned judgment would justify the prayer that there might be a few more philosophers as well as more engineers.

We may well agree that, in one way or another, the development of our human resources is a matter of paramount concern to the nation as a whole, with special emphasis on the immediate need for a greatly increased number of scientifically and technically trained graduates. In accepting this as an immediate responsibility of the University, we must avoid at all costs the tendency to become merely a larger group of larger professional schools. The pressures in this direction are real and the forces at work substantial. They must be resisted. Our policy, then, will be to expand all our professional schools, where the necessity is demonstrated, to the limit of our circumstances. But that expansion must be kept in balance with the expansion of the University as a whole. It must be an expansion with and within the University.

Our aim must be to produce in larger numbers what, for lack of a better term, might be described as better educated individuals. What methods are we to adopt to achieve this purpose? This problem is one for the academic authorities, who know that no mere shuffling of curricula, no casual contacts with the teaching in the Faculty of Arts, will suffice.

The problem is common to all universities having professional schools. John Pilley, Professor of Education in the University of Edinburgh, states it in clear terms in his article in the February, 1957, *Universities Quarterly*:

The teaching that is needed is the kind that will give students the power of interpreting the texts they study, and of comprehending what sort of an activity they are entering into in each of their studies and how these differ from one another. If we could teach all students to read in this sense we should have done a good deal to further their education: unless we can teach our technologists to do it we shall not be doing what we should towards making them either good technologists or educated citizens.

If we are to produce technologists who are educated men we must look not only to what can be done in the universities but also to what can and should be done in the schools. If young people's schooling be effectively liberal it will have given them some experience of what it is to augment their knowledge of themselves and the excitement that goes with it. Specialisation contributes to this end if the specialisation is begun in the way a good sixth form teacher seeks to do it. What is to-day working to prevent the schools from teaching their pupils the art of independent study is the ever earlier, and ever more intense, unreflective specialisation which is required of them. This transforms what should be humanising studies into the learning of subject matter and forces increasingly the adoption of cramming methods. A large part of the blame for this anti-educational development lies with the universities, all too many of whose members share [the] opinion that the school is the place where you obediently learn the facts, and that you only begin to think about them when you get to a university. Until the universities recognise the mischievousness of this view and adopt entrance requirements that give the schools a great deal more enlightened help than they now give in laying the foundations of their pupils' liberal education, no endeavour of [the universities] to produce technologists who are "like any other well educated person" is likely to have any great success.

This, I believe, has some application to our situation. It is not impossible that the adoption of a common first year for all the professional schools might have much to recommend it. There would be advantages in economy, not only in money but in the utilization of space; if, as some would contend, a common first year provides advantages for the development of better educated individuals, it should be seriously considered.

I find myself so much in agreement with Dr. Sidney Smith's address, "The Unity of Knowledge," given before the Royal Canadian Institute on February 23, 1952, that I feel it could well set the direction of academic policy in this respect. Dr. Smith illustrated his plea for the unity of knowledge by quoting from Sir Robert Falconer, who appreciated clearly the different approaches of humanist and scientist, and whose grasp of the new dimension added to higher education by science, and of what Huxley calls "the divine dipsomania of the original investigator," was firm and sure.

*

We are fortunate indeed that the structure of the University of Toronto as it stands today creates no obstacle to the accomplishment of our purposes. Too little credit has been given to the Royal Commission of 1906. This Commission, under the chairmanship of Sir Joseph Flavelle, was charged with an examination of the affairs of the University, and it is from its wise recommendations that the present University Act has evolved.

This Act imposes upon the Board of Governors the task of governing the University, and, at the same time, the responsibility for the appointment of the President of the University. The President, with his academic colleagues, is wholly responsible for the academic affairs of the University. The responsibility of the Chairman of the Board relates to the control of money. This makes possible the maximum flexibility in both the administrative and the academic organization. The President, with his colleagues and the Senate, develops and applies the agreed academic policies, with the certain knowledge that the selection of academic staff is, in the last analysis, his exclusive prerogative. The principle of federation adds strength to the whole and to the constituent parts. The federated colleges have contributed greatly to the spirit of the University. A deep and growing understanding continues to strengthen our common purpose. Looking back over some thirteen years during which I have been officially associated with the University, there is no change in the University Act that I can think of which would better equip us to face the problems of the immediate future.

The question of what the size of the University should be has several facets: How many students will seek admission? Where does size begin to affect the quality of teaching? What is an economical maximum number of students from the viewpoint of overhead and administrative costs? The forecasts that now guide our planning suggest that we will be asked to deal with 22,000 to 25,000 students by 1965 or 1967. It is true that these forecasts do not envisage any relief that might be forthcoming if many more technological institutes were established. Nor do they make allowance for the possibility of changing the standards of university admission.

The Board of Governors must take into account all matters that affect the long-term policy of the University, but must, perforce, confine their active detailed planning to shorter periods concerning which they have reasonably accurate information. In 1950, after the post-war bulge, we concluded that we were again in a position to set student-staff ratios that entitled us to feel that the quality of teaching had been restored to a satisfactory level. With this establishment, we are enabled to deal with 10,000 to 11,000 students and maintain the required high quality of teaching. A satisfactory student-staff ratio must govern the establishment of the future.

For several years, we have considered in what direction the University should acquire new land areas. The decision to procure some 26 acres of residential land west of St. George Street and north of College Street was based, in the first instance, on purely administrative economics. It was considered that the administrative and maintenance facilities were located centrally in relation to this area, and were of adequate capacity to serve any new facilities erected thereon. The area becomes, in reality, a part of the present campus, involving a shifting to the westward of the centre of gravity of the University property. The President has concluded that with new facilities in this area the academic staff can meet the challenge of expansion. Under these circumstances, we may well find ourselves dealing, by 1965 or 1967, with a student population of between 22,000 and 25,000, if that be necessary. Though I share to the full the feeling of my academic colleagues that any university can very easily become too large, I do not view the prospect of 25,000 students with dismay.

Besides examining what we want to do, we must determine what we can do. As I have stated earlier, that will depend upon our circumstances, upon the financial support we can obtain. We must look for that support in several directions. Costs are steadily increasing in every phase of the operation of the University, and we have no private loophole of escape from those increasing costs, nor is there any indication that this trend is likely to change.

Income from student fees has declined as a percentage of our total income, while government grants for current expenditures have substantially increased. Education cannot be deferred, and, on current expenditures account, the annual short fall must be made good by government grants. We are indeed fortunate that up to the present time the balance has actually been achieved, and we have been able to keep our heads above water at the present levels of enrolment. That is all we have done: the increased expenditures of the past ten years are not reflected in any great enrichment of what we can offer to the students, either in studies or in amenities.

Our financial survival has so far been the result of a series of happy accidents, rather than of any special policy or design. This past history has elevated thriftiness to the level of a working principle. We have given splendid value for every dollar received, and I for one pray that this sense of thrift will long remain with us.

It is important, however, to distinguish true thrift from false economy, and this must concern us deeply when we consider the salaries of the teaching staff. Academic salaries have for many years lagged behind those of the general community. The quality of the University is merely a reflection of the quality of the academic staff. To hold the present staff and to secure good additional staff is the first duty of the President, and in order to enable him to do this better, we have recently established a new, substantially higher scale of academic salaries. Expenditures on account of salaries in 1957 will be over $7,000,000.

Expansion of the University, prudent and carefully controlled though it must be, will bring with it considerable increases in current expenditures, of which the increased staff salaries are the foremost example. Governments, both provincial and federal, have increased their grants to a marked degree. It may be necessary to increase the students' fees, though any benefit to be found there could easily be offset by the loss of brilliant student material which higher fees might exclude from the University. The indications are that we must lean more and more on the modern patron of the universities—the taxpayer.

At the same time, the demands for capital expenditure will be greatly augmented, and the question that concerns us particularly at this moment is where we shall seek the monies for this capital programme. Government assistance alone would be insufficient. The generous private donor, whose gifts have done so much for us in the past, is becoming, for reasons we all understand, rarer and rarer. We shall need, in addition, the help of industry, of the graduate body, and of the general public.

In seeking public support, this University appears to labour under the very serious handicap of being regarded in some quarters as a state university, tax supported, and therefore in no dire need. In reality, our objectives and our position are not a whit different from those of the other Canadian universities except in scale and potential.

There is a widespread feeling that the University is idle for five or six months each year, and that the staff enjoy a long and carefree holiday. Many suggest that the term could be lengthened by a month or two. Indeed, there are some who think the University staff could well teach eleven months in every year, thus apparently doubling the output of the University. This hopelessly unrealistic view is based on a complete misunderstanding of how the University functions. It is absolutely necessary for the staff to have time for attendance at meetings, writing and research, if they are to continue to be good teachers.

When the expansion is upon us we must be prepared to accept drastic changes in many of our established customs. We may well have to adapt old existing buildings. New buildings must be less costly than many of the present ones. Indeed, such buildings as are now in the planning stage are designed to combine the efficiency of factory buildings with some improvement in appearance. The spacious dignity of Oxford and Cambridge colleges is simply out of our reach. More effective use must be made of our facilities. In the past, our buildings have, in a sense, belonged to a particular faculty or department. In future there will be a more common and more constant use of these traditionally private lecture rooms, laboratories, and auditoriums. Many plans are under way to improve substantially the utilization of our facilities, and more will be heard of these in the days to come.

With every measure of economy that we can devise, the cost of expansion will still be heavy. I have said, and I am convinced, that we must look for money in several directions. We could ask the government to pay for it all; but in the first place it is highly unlikely that they would do so; and in the second place it would be a very dangerous action for the present Board of Governors to impose upon a historically independent university a legacy of complete dependence on the government of the day. The financing of universities by the state creates unique problems. Despite our happy circumstances here, it would be folly to ignore the possibility of the state's seeking to follow its money and exert influence upon the teaching in the University. It has happened before; indeed, it appears to be happening today in South Africa. Academic freedom is vital to the life of any university, and we must be concerned with anything that appears to threaten it. On the other hand, to refuse state support altogether would mean, under today's conditions, the disappearance of the University. There are many who would prefer to be a live mouse rather than a dead lion. We have to attempt to be a live lion.

The best guarantee against undesirable government interference is to be found in the existence of a wide constituency of loyal graduates interested in the University. Although we have some 69,000 living graduates, it is recognized that much remains to be done to awaken them to the necessity of taking an increased interest in the welfare of their Alma Mater. There is an obvious need to improve our communications with our graduates, as well as with business (whose need for future graduates involves a vital interest in the health of the University), and with the public generally.

University administration is, to some extent, a routine task. It is, however, a task of some magnitude. It carries the responsibility for supervising and controlling the disbursement of some $20,000,000 in academic and non-academic expenditures during each year. It is not an end in itself. It exists only to service and support the academic undertakings. The Board must make the final decisions; they must face the fact that there will never be enough money to give every academic division everything that is needed. After getting the best advice and considering as wisely as they are able, they must be the final arbiter of financial questions—they are the ones who must say Yes, or Partly, or Perhaps, or No.

The view of the future, as I see it from the Board Room window, is full of interest and challenge. While there is now wide agreement as to the general direction of our road, there will be many differences of opinion and much debate on matters of detail.

The Value of the Humanities ▬ *M. St.A. Woodside*

It is comforting for a humanist to reflect upon the well-known words of John Wilson, alias Christopher North, "Animosities are mortal, but the Humanities live forever." A few extremists may urge that there is more of the darkness of night than of the warmth of Ambrose's tavern in the remark, but humanists who have had experience of concentrated attacks on certain areas of their domain will cling to the promise of a day when hostility will vanish and the value of the Humanities will not be questioned. The immortality claimed for the Humanities in *Noctes Ambrosianae* is not open to doubt unless human nature suffers in the future a change such as has not occurred during the centuries of evolution and revolution known to history. It is perhaps safe to assume that until such a radical change does occur, men and women will find their understanding widened and their spirit deepened by Aeschylus, Shakespeare, and Goethe, by Rembrandt and Beethoven; they will reflect upon the meaning of "right" and of "good," of "freedom" and of "truth," and will profit by the reflections of the truly great thinkers of the past and present; they will be intrigued by the processes which have led to social success and failure, to the development of "higher religions," and to the building of the imposing structure of modern science both in its pure and in its applied aspects. Even in the mid-twentieth century, when shorter working hours and rapidity of transportation and communication seem to have had the effect of setting a high premium on leisure, serious novels are published; great playwrights, including Shakespeare and Sophocles, enjoy success; Toynbee's *Study of History* is not only talked about but read; and the philosophers are regarded as worthy companions, especially if one is formally introduced to them by a Will Durant or some other mutual friend. Admittedly it is a minority which displays this interest in the Humanities. Figures are not available, and probably never will be available, to show whether the minority is, proportionately, shrinking or growing; indeed, it is impossible to *measure* the extent, in breadth and depth, of interest in the Humanities. It is reasonable to assert, however, that they still have a very significant place in "our way of life" and that their immortality is not as yet in jeopardy.

What, then, of the "plight of the Humanities"? What is the meaning of the phrase which has, at least until very recently, been almost a *cliché* in discussions about education and about culture generally? It is true that society through various agencies has been willing to provide funds for scientific study and research on a comparatively large scale and that increasingly large numbers of students have been adopting science as their field of study. It is true, also, that today everyone is aware of the critical shortage of teachers of science and not nearly so conscious of the growing shortage in other disciplines. The present situation might well have been foreseen by a moderately gifted prophet. The exhilarating progress of science and the exciting opportunities for scientists have naturally attracted young men and women. A society which is more and more supported by science must stimulate the production of scientists and the development of science. The magnitude of the need and the tremendous speed with which it has grown have naturally created shortages. It would, of course, be quite wrong to assert that a mathematician or a chemist or an engineer or an economic theorist who has received no formal courses in humanistic disciplines at school or university will normally be devoid of any real interest in the Humanities or of any true concern for what they stand for. The bridge-building barbarian and the illiterate industrialist are, it would seem, rare creatures in 1957. The danger is, to put it in extreme terms, that outside pressures, created by a desire for immediate returns, may deprive the student of an opportunity to realize the humanistic interests which he possesses, at least potentially, may cause him to stifle such interests as they begin to develop, and may encourage him to regard any exploitation of such interests as of third-rate importance. Whether or not this now hypothetical danger is to become real depends first on the demands which the Humanities are to be allowed to make on a student's time and energy while he is being educated, and second, on the kind of education which that area of society in which he is to find employment and live his life is to demand of him. Unless these demands are sound, our society takes the risk of cutting itself off from its roots and from any understanding of human values. It thus takes the risk of commiting suicide. An attempt is made in part II which follows to analyse some important aspects of the Humanities; and in part III, to suggest the significance of the Humanities for the modern business world.

II

So much has been written and spoken about the Humanities that it is rash in the extreme to believe that something new and fresh and significant can be said of them. Nevertheless anyone who has the hardihood to essay the almost impossible task must begin by providing some kind of definition or description. The word "Humanities" itself (going back to the Latin "humanitas") has had so long a history, and has been used to convey so many meanings, that no single definition would be universally acceptable. Consequently, for the sake of clarity, anyone who uses the term in debate must state as convincingly as possible the meaning which is attached to it.

Exactly what Cicero himself meant by "humanitas" is not yet clear and perhaps for present purposes it does not matter much. Only a thoroughly convinced humanist would accept the light from so remote a past as an illumination of present discussion. The humanistic movement of the fifteenth century (in Western Europe) "broke through the mediaeval traditions of scholastic theology and philosophy and devoted itself exclusively to the rediscovery and direct study of the ancient classics. This movement was essentially a revolt against intellectual, and especially ecclesiastical, authority and is the parent of all modern developments whether intellectual, scientific or social." Any physical or social scientist who will accept a judgment embedded in an unsigned article in the *Encyclopedia Britannica* will recognize that, historically, it was the humanists who gave him his freedom. At the same time it should be noted that scholastic philosophy and religion (or at any rate the history of religion) are now accepted as component parts of the "Humanities." Somewhat later, in the Battle of the Books, there was a struggle between the ancient classics, that is, the Humanities *par excellence*, and modern works written in vernacular languages. That struggle has ended and both ancient and modern books will be found without distinction in the libraries of undoubted humanists. These two examples —and that is all they are—taken from the history of the "Humanities" will serve to indicate that the Humanities do not represent a body of fixed and unchanging dogma. On the contrary, it is characteristic of them not to be restricted by "laws." They have had the capacity to grow as society and its interests have grown and to develop both by absorbing old enemies and by accepting antagonists as allies. Rightly considered, they are dynamic rather than static, and accretive rather than exclusive. The Greek and Latin classics still belong to the Humanities, but a

Renaissance humanist would be surprised, and perhaps shocked, to discover how much else has been added to their strength.

It is perhaps true to say that one of the causes, or indeed the main cause, of the flexibility and "progressiveness" which mark the Humanities properly considered is the fact that the disciplines which are grouped under the broad term are largely subjective. In the realm of the Humanities subjectivity is paradoxically the glory and strength of the student and at the same time his weakness. It is not his purpose to arrive at "laws," convenient though it may be from time to time to use the term, but to produce judgments based on rational arguments. He must strive, therefore, to beware of any perversion of his argument and of any warping of his judgment by personal idiosyncrasies. At the same time he must recognize that he lacks and probably always will lack the means of the scientist to make accurate measurements and to test hypotheses experimentally. Ultimately he must depend upon himself, with such help as he can obtain from colleagues—that is, from others interested in the same subject-matter—and even when help is provided by colleagues, he alone can judge the validity of what they are able to offer. The "research team," whatever success it may or may not have had in other areas, can produce only limited results in humanistic investigation. This is true of literature, philosophy, and history in all its branches. To take history as a specific example, there is no set of purely objective facts which the student may and must accept. All that exists is "historical evidence," the marks on paper or stone or canvas, the objects, and the oral tradition which the past has left behind. The historian does the best he can with the evidence, but all he can do is to provide others with his inevitably subjective experience in studying this fragmentary and principally dumb material. Consequently, the serious reader of history cannot, if he is wise, accept uncritically and make his own, for example, the judgment, "Napoleon was a blight on Europe," just because an historian of note has made it. He must come to his own conclusion by whatever routes are available to him. Similarly, although religion and philosophy may give invaluable stimulus, each human individual must reach his own explanation of "right" and "wrong." The subjectivity of the Humanities has two important results. First, it ensures the timelessness of the great humanistic productions. The scientist cannot profit scientifically by studying Greek science of the fifth and fourth centuries B.C. because science has objective standards and the science of that age is out of date. But Thucydides and Shakespeare and Kant are not out of date because in their works the perennial problems of human beings are analysed by men of outstanding genius and, in the cases of Thucydides and Shakespeare, with consummate art. The problems attacked by science can be solved with at least some measure of finality; the large problems in which humanists as such are interested have not yet been solved except in so far as individuals have solved them for themselves, but they have been clearly established and brilliantly attacked by a succession of great and lucid minds. And second, the student of the Humanities, whether professional or not, will, unless he is totally cut off from the contemporary world, reflect in his interests and in his choice of subject-matter the interests of his age. Thus the specific subject-matter adopted by the humanist changes from age to age. Examples are not far to seek. The Humanities today include the literatures, history, and philosophies of the Middle and Far East; the history and philosophy of science are investigated; the original humanists, the classicists, are studying the economic life of the ancient world for the first time.

How is it possible accurately to define or describe this flexible and apparently almost elusive group of disciplines? One must resort to qualification and ultimately to arbitrariness. "All recorded signs of what man has found in himself and in the world about him are brought within the disciplines of the Humanities to be given form by scholars and teachers for use by all men in present and in future times," writes David H. Stevens in *The Changing Humanities*. This able definition (or description) would seem to include among the Humanities science, mathematics, and the social sciences, and even, from the other pole, quackery and superstition. In limited measure its inclusiveness is quite proper. "The Humanities deal with *all* those aspects and achievements of man which make him man as distinguished from the animals or from God." In the "Report of a Special Committee on the Humanities Appointed by the President of the University of Toronto" (1954) this point is developed: the Humanities "rightly involve the study of man's environment for man cannot be divorced from his physical, social and spiritual surroundings. But the emphasis is laid upon man rather than upon the environment. Man is at the centre; the environment is his setting, his challenge, his stimulus, one of his problems." If man, reacting to the challenge of his environment, develops science or theology or a complicated social and economic structure or even superstition, the humanist must be interested in the process. In modern academic terms, the history of science and of religion, economic history and social history, the history of alchemy and of witchcraft belong to the Humanities, while science, theology, economics, and witchcraft, purely considered, do not.

As has been suggested above, it is difficult to draw a definite boundary line. Part of the difficulty is due to the fact that most, if not all, scientists, social scientists, and applied scientists are humanists as well as scientists, whether or not they have "taken courses" in humanistic subjects, and that it is practically impossible to divide their activities as scientists and as humanists into water-tight compartments. (The same may, of course, be said of men in walks of life other than the sciences, but the common academic divisions of Science, Social Science, and Humanities are at present convenient.) This blurring of boundaries extends to disciplines as well as to individuals. Anthropology, political science, and sociology, all social sciences, are in some aspects closely akin to history, a humanity; while political science in its theoretical aspects is essentially philosophy. History itself is sometimes numbered among the Humanities, sometimes among the Social Sciences. However, as the "Report" says, "All the sciences are neutral with regard to values. Judgments on values are characteristic of the Humanities." The sciences limit themselves to saying, "This is so." The Humanities freely say, "This is good"; or "This is ugly." It is sometimes urged that the sciences are vitally concerned with one value, namely truth. But truth is the guiding star of all disciplines, subjective or objective. Without it there would be no disciplines. All disciplines live in the atmosphere of truth. And it is a special task of philosophy, one of the Humanities, to examine the nature of truth itself. It is possible to go further and point out that certain subjects of study commonly included among the Humanities have no real affinities with them. Some aspects of pure linguistic study do not seem properly to belong. Textual criticism, epigraphy, and papyrology in certain of their phases seem remote. They are all valid forms of scholarly activity, but humanities only in so far as they serve the needs of the humanist proper.

The disciplines which will be assigned by present arbitrary disposal to the Humanities are undoubtedly already apparent: Language as a medium of human communication and expression, Literature, Art and Music, Philosophy, History, including the history of science, the history of art, the history of religion, and economic history. They are all somehow concerned with man's inner needs, his problems, his aspirations, his successes, and his failures; in short, with the amazingly incalculable human spirit. At their best, within the area which is theirs, they offer a broadening of the understanding and a fortification of the spirit.

Are they always at their best? It would be odd if they were because they are of necessity in the charge of men and women and live only within the confines of human minds. One fancies that the prestige and the usefulness of the Humanities have often suffered through wilful or careless mistreatment which makes the Humanities appear to be other than they are. Three examples may be cited, one from each of three levels in our educational system.

(a) The Greek and Latin classics, and the languages in which they are written, have borne the brunt of most attacks based on the alleged uselessness of the Humanities. The correct defence is that the Greek and Roman civilization produced a body of humanistic literature second to none in quantity and quality and superior to most, and that the men of genius who created this literature discussed with clarity, and often with great art, every major human problem. The Greek and Latin languages are studied to give us access to this magnificent literature; translations are a poor second best because the process of translation at its most skilful replaces the art of the author by the quite different art of the translator, destroys the flavour of the original, and often reduces its delicate precision. (The age of electronics promises us translating-machines. Whatever machines may do for a technical article on physics, one shudders to think of the murder they would commit on a speech by Thucydides or an ode of Horace.) The defence established, another attack is delivered. "High school students are unable to read Greek and Latin fluently enough for the classics when they leave school; they never really gain access to this wonderful body of literature; their time has been wasted." The defenders of the garrison are dismayed by this counter-attack. Instead of saying, "We have given the rudiments of the subject to these students; they are capable, if they have the will and the taste, of pursuing these studies further, either formally or informally, and of shortly entering the realm to which we have given them the pass-port," they take refuge in what are for the public unconvincing arguments. Latin and Greek improve one's English. Latin and Greek help one to understand words. Latin and Greek have a beneficial effect on one's logical processes. It is perfectly true that a study of Latin and Greek can have these effects. But they are *by-products*, not the reason for a study of Latin and Greek, and the public is thoroughly aware of it. Unfortunately for the classicists the public does not attack, for example, Mathematics in the same way although Mathematics is equally vulnerable. The present writer never *used* his Grade XIII Mathematics until his son encountered minor mathematical difficulties at high school. He enjoyed it for what it was to him, profited by the by-products, and rejoiced that he had proceeded a short distance to a kingdom which he would probably never enter. The public is inconsistent. Mathematics, it says, is useful and Classics is not. But it has jockeyed the classicists into a position where they are obliged to stress the *minutiae* of language, to fix their eyes on the means rather than the end. The universities share a measure of blame with the public. They naturally expect that students from the schools who propose to embark on a formal study of Greek and Latin literature should have done a great deal of the donkey-work in grammar and vocabulary before they reach the universities. For the sake of the few who do proceed formally with classical studies, their influence, gentle though it may be, forces the majority to accept a means as an end. Is it not possible, within four or five years, to come closer to providing a high-school student with a *reading* knowledge of Latin and Greek and at the same time to introduce him to a great humanistic document in its entirety—the *Iliad*, for example, or the *Aeneid* ? If I were an employer and were obliged to make a highly difficult choice, I would be inclined to accept an applicant who had an understanding of the *Odyssey* as a whole rather than one who had read Book IX in Greek, could transpose all the queer Homeric forms into their Attic counterparts, and had never heard of the remaining twenty-three books. Fortunately it is at least possible that such a choice may be avoided. With encouragement from the universities and from society, a high-school student might at the same time be given a start on a reading knowledge of Latin, devoid of any major claim to philological erudition, and at the same time an appreciation appropriate to an adolescent (and that is high appreciation: the writer has over a period of nearly thirty years read the *Odyssey* in Butcher and Lang's or E. V. Rieu's translation to a large number of boys and girls varying in age from seven to fourteen years, including his own hypercritical sons; the enthusiasm and appreciation have been extraordinary) of at least one great humanistic document created by the Greeks and Romans. To be fair to the universities it must be stated that their undergraduate departments are also under pressure. A. N. Whitehead has somewhere said that classical teaching "is obsessed with the formation of finished classical scholars." In some measure the classicists have forgotten the Bachelor of Arts who proposes to invest his life in commerce or one of the learned professions exclusive of teaching, and have used as a criterion in establishing courses of study, the demands of faculties of graduate studies.

(*b*) English Language and Literature is taken as the second example, this time of the undergraduate level. In the professional faculties of many universities, English Literature (with or without Composition) is accepted as a required discipline. The humanist's heart is encouraged and he lifts up his downcast eyes. However, if he discreetly probes within a given faculty, he may discover, at least from some members, that Chaucer and Milton and Shaw (Shakespeare enjoying immunity from criticism by virtue of extraordinary prestige) are not really what is desired. The essays of Bacon and Hazlitt are not much better. "English" has been included in the curriculum because students are unable to write cogent and well-organized reports. But Milton and Hazlitt are so remote from modern speech and their subject-matter is so unattractive that they are not really practical. The social sciences are in the same case. Psychology, or a short course therein, is included because professional people usually have dealings with human beings; political science, because professional people often come in contact with government. What seems to be required is not wisdom or depth of understanding or an illumination of the soul, but a kind of technical proficiency. This is not too bad if in fact the great pieces of English literature are used as the means to the end because in this case the means may, with skilful treatment, become the end. But there is evidence enough to show that often humane studies are regarded as technical training. Try to persuade the members of a professional faculty to accept, let us say, the *Oresteia* of Aeschylus, an incredibly great trilogy of tragedies, as a course for their students and the exact meaning of the present argument will probably become apparent.

(c) The final example is taken from the high level of postgraduate teaching and research. A discipline with widespread boundaries, especially in an age of expanding scholarship, is characterized by specialization, and specialization has been carried to the usual length in the Humanities. For example, each of the Cambridge *Histories*, which form one of the great monuments of modern scholarship, is not really a *history* at all, but a collection of monographs by specialists arranged chronologically and bound together in a number of volumes. In the universities there is pressure on professors to publish, and on graduate students to write Ph.D. theses. The result has been a tendency to look for raw material which has not been exploited and to work up small portions of it for publication. This is not improper activity and, given existing circumstances, it is almost inevitable. Theoretically, great works of synthesis will appear from time to time and the relevance of the short articles on comparatively small points will be made plain. Works of synthesis, however, are rare. And the interested and intelligent layman conceives the opinion that professional humanists are more interested in what has not been done than in what ought to be done, and can be done with humanistic profit. The interpretation of a chorus by Sophocles surely has more relevance, humanistically speaking, than the elucidation of a fragmentary commercial contract on papyrus from an Egyptian rubbish heap. In fact both kinds of investigation should be undertaken. A quick survey of the learned journals devoted to the Humanities will suggest that much more time and energy is being given to individual leaves on individual branches than to the trees or to the forest itself.

The criticism of the Humanities in practice, offered above, should not mislead the reader into a belief that the present writer doubts their great value. If he were entering the University again, he would again elect the study of the Humanities and more specifically, the study of the Greek and Latin classics. The criticism is that of a husband who regards his wife as the most wonderful of God's creations and who criticizes her choice in hats and dresses, not because they make her any less wonderful in fact, but because they give the public the impression that she is not as wonderful as she really is.

III

One of the important facts about the twentieth century is that within its first fifty years the businessman, in the widest meaning of the term, has become the heir of all ancient aristocracies, challenged for pride of place only by the professional athlete and the professional entertainer, and challenged by them only in very small degree. Within his own community, whether it be small or large, he is at once the prop and stay of almost everything, and the leader in almost every worthy enterprise. National governments and international organizations seek his advice and his support. He is the modern patron of art, music, and the drama. Without him scientific research would languish. And in addition to all this, the physical and social welfare of millions of individual human beings depends on his knowledge, his wisdom, and his judgment. Whether or not he has sought it, history has assigned to him a role of tremendous responsibility. Every thinking member of society is vitally interested in the capacities of the businessman and the means by which his capacities have been developed.

Nobody would deny in A.D. 1957 that an educated man should have at least some understanding of the methods and principles and limitations of the Sciences and of the Social Sciences. A senior officer of a large Canadian corporation recently suggested publicly that it is just as important for a cultivated man to have some knowledge of the working of a modern joint-stock company as of the Greek city-state. With this no true humanist would disagree. But whereas it is customary to accept, as important, the claims of physics or economics on the attention of the would-be educated man, it is not unusual to hear the claims of literature and philosophy denied. Is there any justifiable place, in the education of the businessman, for the subjects termed "Humanities"?

A businessman is, in addition to being an executive officer, or a manager, or a promoter, or anything else, a human being, and as such he is the victim or the product of essentially human needs and aspirations. He is not a hermit. On the contrary he is in hourly contact with colleagues, assistants, technical experts, foremen, employees, and secretaries, each of whom is, at least in theory, *homo sapiens*, even before he is *homo mechanicus, homo economicus*, or *homo quidlibet*, and each of whom has the same human needs and aspirations as the businessman *par excellence*. Can it be said that a knowledge and understanding of needs, aspirations, and values are unimportant or impractical? Is it possible to delegate such knowledge and understanding to personnel officers and public relations experts without loss? The great difficulty, of course, is that it is absolutely impossible to measure, even in rough terms, the advantage accruing to a businessman through a grasp of the Humanities, to compute the value of self-knowledge, of knowledge of the common measure of all human beings.

In recent times university placement officers and others have reported a desire on the part of commerce and industry to recruit university graduates with a "general degree" and have hinted that there is a demand for men and women with a broad educational background. Since businessmen have apparently adopted this attitude themselves, it is doubtless derived from experience, and one guesses that it is in some measure a recognition of the desirability of a basic education which can be valid in a variety of specific situations. There is here no suggestion at all that disciplines other than the Humanities are not broad and basic. Economics and political science, for example, can be broad and basic, whereas specific training for one kind of commerce or industry is not and tends towards technical training. The contention is that the Humanities rightly regarded and rightly pursued can produce a flexibility of mind and an understanding which should enable an individual, even when he has only himself to depend on, to attack a problem involving human beings in a reasonably effective manner.

At the moment there is serious apprehension that we shall be unable to defend our "way of life" against an attack of some kind supported by the growing scientific and technological proficiency of others who do not accept this way. Apprehension leads to a profound worry that our scientific and technological growth is lagging behind that of our opponents and from time to time one can detect in some quarters a disposition somehow to channel our human resources into applied science and technology and if necessary to sacrifice study in other areas. What is this "way of life" which is so precious? It is a complex tangle of values resulting from a long and complicated historical process. It is easy to make phrases about it and to juggle the *clichés*. All known disciplines are required for a full and clear understanding of it, but without the humanistic disciplines success is impossible. The very terms "democracy" and "freedom" admit of no simple definition or description; what the terms stand for must be earned daily by the fortunate possessors, and can be effectively defended, without grave damage to themselves, only by those who understand them. Is there any profit in trying to protect our "way of life" if the means which we adopt bring it into jeopardy? We must try to understand ourselves. Furthermore, we must try to understand others. The well-advertised shrinking of the world has brought us into close contact with millions of fellow-humans whose "way of life" is not ours and who look upon us with suspicion occasionally tinged with jealousy of our material (not our spiritual) resources. They are potentially our collaborators in the construction of a finer world society; they are also potentially our enemies. Our great weakness is an almost total lack of understanding of them and their values. We cannot speak their language either literally or figuratively. There is no short-cut to this priceless understanding. The peoples of Southeast Asia, or of the Middle East, or of the Slavic-speaking world are beyond the reach of our understanding until we understand their literatures, their history, and their philosophies. This is one of the large modern tasks of the Humanities, and it is one in which the businessman as well as all other members of our Western community must participate in some measure. Success will be good for business; it will also be good for human society. Eventually we will learn, perhaps painfully, that friendship cannot be bought. It is won, and it is won by friendly understanding.

It is hoped that for their own sake, as well as for that of the community which they lead, the new aristocrats—the businessmen—will be able, while of necessity keeping an eye on present problems, to take the responsibility of adopting a long view. *Quidquid agas, prudenter agas et respice finem.*

Universities and the Making of Businessmen

Sir Arnold Plant

Universities are the home
of vocational education. Throughout the greater part of their history,
the task of the most ancient of them was to educate men for the
ecclesiastical profession, including the public and civil offices to which
clerics then expected as of right to be nominated. I recall the impression
made upon me by a passage in a paper delivered in 1921 by the late
Sir William Ashley, then Professor of Commerce and Vice-Principal
of the University of Birmingham, to the Second Conference of Universities of the Empire assembled at Oxford. "It may be doubted," he said,
"whether general mental culture was ever maintained to be the prime
raison d'être of a university until Oxford and Cambridge, some sixty
or seventy years ago, began to acquire a body of resident lay tutors. In
encouraging what we may even call 'vocational' studies, the modern
university is but reverting to its age-long traditions." As I had myself
a year earlier interrupted (as I then imagined) my career as a business
manager to study at a university in preparation for more responsible
administrative work, it was reassuring to learn that in preferring the
economics and commerce degree curricula at London to the best alternatives which, as it seemed to my untutored mind, the older universities
then had to offer, I had probably chosen even better than I knew. I was
already finding my capacities more than sufficiently extended by my
studies and the calls of student life in London. Vocational subjects
directly and obviously appropriate to a business career were handled
in a way which developed and exercised the reasoning faculty, providing
the mental discipline and mental enlargement which merits the name
of a university education.

So at any rate it has seemed to me. I cannot of course know whether
the path I chose was in fact the best then open to me. I know only that

I went through the anxieties of mental torment. The process is familiar enough to those who have been privileged to pursue any well-organized course of study in one of the real universities of the world. I remember first one's consternation at being unable to see that intellectual problems and difficulties existed which clearly worried fellow students and teachers whom one had already learned to respect. Then came the flash of realization, the effort to define a problem, once perceived, in terms which pinned it down, and the baffling failure to find a satisfying path towards its solution. Occasionally there followed the infuriating assistance from a book or a teacher which revealed one's stupidity. More often than not the chase had to be adjourned at the stage when one knew little more than what were the fallacious or sterile approaches to the solution, and realized that a great deal more reading, research, and reflection had to be undertaken before one could hope to make a confident step forward. My vocational course of study was exquisite torture, culminating in a self-imposed life sentence of hard intellectual labour.

The fact that the development of new specialist schools of learning in response to changing social and industrial needs came more quickly in England in the universities of the metropolis and the growing provincial centres than in the older universities was due at least as much to their special interest in opportunist experimentation as to any sure conviction that what they proposed to offer was intellectually more suitable for the more able students or more satisfying to every teacher. After all, the newer universities had of necessity in the early stages of their development to attract their own teachers from the ancient centres, and these men knew that a curriculum which failed to impart a general mental culture had no place in a university. The older universities continued to develop their schools and triposes along the old and well-tested lines which most surely achieved that main purpose. The college fellows concentrated on teaching what they understood, building on the subjects traditionally taught in the famous schools from which they themselves were largely drawn and to which they looked for their most typical students. It was a self-perpetuating sequence in which the art of thought was transmitted by scholar-teachers to scholar-pupils, some of who hoped to remain as teachers, or at worst to become teachers elsewhere. The rest went out into a somewhat remote and strange world to apply their trained minds to mundane affairs, confident if they were good scholars that, like lawyers who accept briefs relating to intricate patent litigation, they could quickly call for, assemble, and master the significant data and apprehend and apply the basic principles of the relevant technologies to any problem that came to hand.

To such scholars at the older universities a century ago, and indeed more recently, suggestions that they should extend their teaching interests to the creation of new "subjects," catering even in a tentative and experimental way for the emergent needs of the new applied sciences and technologies, or for the specialist applications of formal logic and philosophical reasoning in the field of economic analysis and the social sciences, were entertained with caution. A Greats teacher might find it a diverting intellectual exercise to write a paper or a treatise on the principles of political economy, a mathematician might amuse himself on an excursion into the less precise field of statistical probability, a natural scientist into bio-chemistry or strength of materials, and so on. The announcement of a course of special lectures, perhaps in a university extension programme, would provide the necessary stimulus to writing and the opportunity to try out a manuscript before publication. A specialist course of lectures which aroused sufficient interest among the student body and controversy between dons might be repeated with appropriate embellishments. But the young ambitious Fellow who wished to concentrate on developing a new "subject" in his college and university would have to weigh the odds very carefully. He would have to turn aside from one of the main streams of scholarly interest and support: his college might object to his withdrawal from traditional teaching duties. He might negotiate an outside endowment to finance a special post, in the hope that the university authority could be prevailed upon to accept it and that he himself might be so fortunate in due course as to be elected to occupy it. He could then specialize in his research; but to be sure of good students, he would need to get the new subject recognized by the university for inclusion as an optional paper in a traditional degree examination, and if the new field of learning was capable of being adequately developed by nothing less than a group of specialized subjects comprising an entirely new degree school or tripos he might well find himself engaged in a life-long and fierce intellectual controversy at the highest level of university politics.

To ambitious young specialist dons, the developing new universities offered a welcome short-cut to the life of specialized research and teaching which they sought. They hoped to take with them the aims and ideals but not the shackles of the traditions in which they had been nurtured, and the governing bodies of the new universities had, as I have said, their own special reasons for providing the opportunities which the migrant scholars required. The metropolis and the rapidly growing provincial centres of population needed their own university colleges, certainly, to cater in the traditional subjects of higher education for students who, for reasons of intellectual quality or financial circumstance or other limitations which have ceased to be relevant, were unable to gain admission to the older universities. But that in itself offered a not very exciting future. On the other hand, each centre had its own new and clamant needs. The rapid progress of scientific discovery and its exploitation by the new technologies, the industrial revolution, the transport development which extended so rapidly the search for new materials and the demand for competent linguists, the need for more and more specialized staff in expanding business, and social and civil needs for school teachers, doctors, hospital specialists and government officials: these and similar demands presented to the new universities an exciting opportunity for pioneer development accompanied by offers of conditional financial support and special endowment. In response to these frankly utilitarian demands, specialist chairs and lectureships were established, new subjects added to the curricula, and new faculties and degree courses created. Not all of the demands and offers of financial support were of the kind that could properly be entertained by a university, but it is noteworthy that comparatively few mistakes were made, and today there are, I imagine, not many scholars left in the university world who would deny that a curriculum aiming directly at utility in the choice of fields of study can, if the subjects are taught in the right way, provide the general mental discipline and enlargement which it is the purpose of a university to impart to its students.

Today the differences in scope which until recently distinguished the curricula of the older and the newer universities have largely disappeared. As new faculties established their claim to permanence, parallel developments were introduced in their own way by Oxford and Cambridge. For instance, Greats scholars were sent elsewhere to study economics, to teach the subject in Oxford on their return, and the economics school was strengthened by recruitment from the newer universities. Today it is one of the leading centres of economics teaching. Once a wider diversification of intellectual endeavour had been secured, the resistance to innovation was weakened, and there is now a healthy rivalry to introduce new academic disciplines in all centres. It is, however, noteworthy that in neither Oxford nor Cambridge has provision yet been made in the economics faculties for teaching in accounting, a field of study in which unsettled economic problems of great intellectual interest abound. Statistics as a subject is better served.

II

It is high time that I turned to the place which universities now occupy, and in which as I see it they are destined to play an increasingly important role, in education and training for careers in business.

I am concerned here with those who transact business and manage concerns, in both the private and the public sectors of the economy, and not with the technological staffs employed by business, except in so far as they participate in business administration. As the universities broadened and intensified their research and teaching activities in the natural and applied sciences, engineering, industrial chemistry, and the various fields of technology, they became at once an indispensable, and by and large the main, source from which industry draws the technologists whose specialization stems from a sound education and training in fundamental scientific principles and research. (In this context I ignore the constitutional demarcations which in some parts of Europe allocate these fields of "university" work to Polytechnics, technische Hochschulen, and the like.) Professional institutes also have developed their own systems of examination for membership side by side with, and sometimes in advance of, the universities, but on the whole a close co-operation and collaboration has been maintained. Their activities are complementary and not seriously disturbed by fundamental conflict or controversy.

In the fields of business in which specialization has in practice assumed a professional or quasi-professional character, evolution has followed a somewhat similar pattern. Banking, insurance (particularly in the actuarial and financial fields), accountancy, commercial law, and company secretarial practice are outstanding instances. Encouraged by employers, institutes have been established to develop examination systems leading to special professional qualifications. The provision of education in preparation for examination is not normally, however, among their objects, and in the United Kingdom the universities have not taken the lead in offering comprehensive courses of study designed to cover these professional requirements. That has been for a number of reasons. In the first place, the examinations are designed primarily for persons already in full-time employment, while even the newer universities cater primarily for full-time students. Second, the conditions for membership of the institutes normally require a minimum period of practical experience in professional duties, if not articled pupilship. Third, the examinations frequently test knowledge of techniques, working rules, and professional practices which, however necessary for practitioners, are not in themselves suitable material on which to organize a course of study which provides a university education. In the result, the great majority of candidates preparing for these examinations have hitherto taken correspondence courses, and the remainder have mostly gone to technical and commercial colleges. The course of events has, however, started a new movement which has already brought the universities and some of these professional bodies into collaboration in ways which will be explained later. The last reason is that until recently the businessmen who employ these professional specialists have not themselves for the most part had personal experience of, or acquaintance with universities and, with some outstanding exceptions, have not expected university graduates as such to be generally employable in their field of business.

Most self-made men are still human, and their complacency easily takes the form of assuming that the way they got on, with little organized education to help them, has much if not everything to be said for it. Early in life they learned the hard way that punctual attendance, short holidays, the cheerful acceptance of menial routine, and the long fatiguing days which made a mockery of leisure hours were the common lot of conscientious young businessmen. They learned later on that, apart from good luck, success depends upon stamina, nerve, and judgment; upon willingness to take big risks, skill in hard-headed buying and selling negotiations, foresight in constructing and equipping production plants, and leadership and human understanding in labour relations. They could hardly be blamed if they imagined that the products of the universities were fastidious young gentlemen, cast in a very different mould and destined by education and training for more sheltered vocations than business management. Certainly many of the sons of self-made men who went to universities preferred afterwards to enter one of the learned professions, rather than their father's or anyone else's business.

During my own adult life two important circumstances have brought about a marked change of attitude in the United Kingdom. One is the proliferation of scholarships and maintenance grants for university students, and the other the Second World War which threw university teachers, businessmen, and civil servants together as never before.

The narrow path from school to university, formerly trodden by the more fortunate of the exceptionally talented youth of the country, has widened into a broad highway for all who can show reasonable capacity to profit from a university education. In consequence, the former methods of recruitment of staff for business concerns and of entrants into the business professions have become obsolete. The state scholarships and grants for university courses of study skim most of the cream of the schools, and more besides. Hitherto an employer who recruited his junior staff direct from school could normally expect, if his methods of selection were reasonably efficient, to catch in his net a fair cross-section of the country's young people, including a good proportion who were deserving of special encouragement and showed promise of fitness for promotion to maintain the succession of efficient management, even in a rapidly expanding business. Now (to revert to the former metaphor) he is liable by such methods to get mainly skimmed milk. The business-man realizes today that had he been born a generation later he would almost certainly himself have gone to a university, and that unless special steps were taken to make a business career at least as attractive as the others open to university men he would have been lost to the business world. There can no longer be any general expectation of maintaining the present level of managerial ability in the hierarchy of a concern by continuing recruitment through the former channels.

Moreover, the need has changed. The general industrial manager today strives to keep abreast of scientific and technological change, to strengthen by new techniques, wider understanding, and improved communication that morale inside his business on which the high productivity of team work depends, and above all to discern and interpret the rapidly changing pattern of the economic and political framework which determines his access to markets and to productive resources, his receipts and outgoings, his profits and his losses. The young manager of our time requires a much wider and higher attainment in general education than was available to his predecessors if he is to grapple successfully with these new complexities. The universities aim to provide what is wanted, and it is in the universities that the more promising of young people are now being educated. Reluctant to do so though some of them may still be, businessmen today look to the universities for most of their successors, and in the search for the talent and qualities they require they are negotiating as never before with the university authorities and teachers.

The post-war years have been highly propitious for planning a combined operation, for war experience has made collaboration easier, more agreeable and rewarding. Until war-time duties threw them together, many of the more able and influential men on both sides knew little from personal contact of the calibre of their new associates. The task of mobilizing the war effort of the country fell upon the departments of government. The administrative civil servants, themselves university men, turned for help partly to their university friends and teachers and partly to leading and experienced practical men of affairs who could organize the production and supply arrangements of the country's business. Both sides emerged richer for the experience, each with a far better opinion of members of the other side as persons and a new respect for their callings and aspirations. Since the war, though businessmen and university dons were at first necessarily preoccupied with the task of getting their former places of work into good running order in new and difficult circumstances, contacts have been maintained. They collaborated in the urgent duty of helping returned service-men to settle into their life's work, and they learned much from that rewarding exercise. Continuing governmental calls upon businessmen and their younger colleagues have afforded ample opportunities for maintaining and extending constructive team work.

At a more formal level, the Federation of British Industries, in conjunction with the Committee of Vice Chancellors and Principals, has promoted in recent years a series of national and regional conferences of industrialists and university men with the express purpose of thinking out the kind of relationships which could best be developed between them in the years to come. These efforts at collaboration have, it is true, borne earlier and better fruit in the context of the education and training of industrial scientists and technologists than in that of making better supply and training arrangements for potential business administrators and department managers. The reason lies in the difference in the nature of the two problems. In the first case, the university product has some immediate and employable utility. In the second, even the best feed-stock must be matured in the right conditions before it has real fitness for purpose, and time and investment alone reveal which of the feed-stock deserves further maturing and which, like some quite respectable and potable wine, is better segregated for earlier consumption at the more modest tables. Where and how the maturing or training process for potential administrators is best arranged is the interesting question.

III

In a paper submitted five years ago to the Nottingham Conference on Industry and the Universities (the report of the Conference was published by the Federation of British Industries), an industrial administrator who was himself a university graduate, Sir Edward Herbert, welcomed happily the fact that the future leaders of industry must largely be drawn from the university students of today. "In these future leaders," he said, "industry will seek a combination of three main categories of ability. The first of these is a man's particular aspect of his firm's business in which he is engaged, so that he may speak, advise and act with genuine authority. . . . It is essential that he shall have studied deeply and successfully during his time at the university. If he has once studied deeply in the early formative years of his life, he has the equipment to do so again. Therefore, I would emphasise the importance of a high academic standard, of a good degree, above all else . . . the tougher and more exact the subject the better." The second ability is to "be able to relate his own specialist function to the conduct of the business as a whole and . . . to keep abreast of current thought in the whole field of management techniques. . . . He must never become so immersed in the problems of his own job, or of his own industry, as to lose sight of the world outside. . . . This capacity to specialise without becoming narrow is always a test of the good administrator." A university course should therefore encourage a man to seek "to extend his awareness of the world in general" and to acquire "some knowledge, at least, of subjects other than its own. . . . Moreover, the student must, somehow, absorb and develop those critical standards of judgement by which he will afterwards avoid magnifying his own personal problems, or the problems which confront him in his job. He will need to learn that men have always been vain, capricious and unwise and that there is nothing in the least surprising in their being so in this twentieth century, however technical, complicated and logical the daily work they do." The task of acquiring perspective can in part be achieved by his cultivating the widest possible range of interests during his time at the university. The third ability required is "that necessary to bear the moral burden of responsibility. He should be ever eager for responsibility and, indeed, somewhat impatient for it . . . he should be prepared in mind and spirit to assume it gladly and without strain. . . . It may be that a man's essential character so governs this question, that his ultimate fitness for responsibility can be revealed only by the long tests of time and opportunity. There are, however, two things that a university ought to do towards forming a man's character in the right mould: it should be able to foster in him a lasting regard for other human beings; and it should strive to instil in him the conceptions of duty and service."

I make no apology for quoting at some length from this, to me, unexceptionable statement. What guidance does it give on the question of the appropriate curricula and organization for university education?

It is, I believe, important to distinguish two streams of university entrants, both of equally high intellectual calibre and promise. One stream is identified by the fact that the students have all set their minds and ambitions on careers as businessmen. The other is made up of those who wish to pursue a particular academic course of study, but are doubtful or quite undecided as to their ultimate vocation.

Many of the students in the former category will wish, and will be well advised, to select a degree curriculum which is specifically designed to cater on sound academic lines for their special interest. In the United Kingdom, the various universities have by now settled down to a broadly similar pattern of first degree in the faculties concerned at an honours level with the social sciences, although the nomenclature differs— B.Sc.Econ., B.Com.(Birmingham), B.A.(Com.), P.P.E.(Modern Greats), and so on. The London B.Sc.Econ. curriculum is not untypical: a Part I which embraces the four main basic fields of economics, history, politics, and possibly law, followed by Part II in which a student may concentrate on industry and trade, or accounting, or on one of a dozen other fields of academic specialization. The great majority of the students who intend to enter business are eager on graduation to obtain immediate appointments as "management trainees" in businesses large enough to require a steady stream of recruits and consequently to maintain an adequate scheme of all-round initiation followed by assignment to a specialized field. As regards the business professions, such as accounting, reference was made in part II of this paper to a new movement which has brought the universities into collaboration with the professional institutes. Accountants have now found that their former recruitment channels for articled pupils direct from the schools no longer bring forward a sufficient number of youths of the right calibre. On the other hand several of the universities today offer degree courses in which accounting, commercial and company law, and the application of economic principles to business finance are studied as fully developed academic subjects. In consequence university graduates who have specialized in these fields are accepted for practical training for reduced periods of articled service, and exemptions are granted from appropriate parts of the professional examinations.

The other stream of students falls again into two categories, sufficiently distinct to call for separate consideration. A significant number of them are attracted to the natural sciences and to engineering, and at the outset are undecided whether their ultimate interest will lie in academic research or in industry, and if in industry whether they will prefer research or other professional work on the one hand or works management and general administration on the other. During their university studies, a number of them will be attracted to the more human side of factory or general management. In London, an inter-collegiate arrangement has been made under which undergraduates in the science and engineering faculties may elect in the later stages of their degree course to combine the study of economics, law, accounting, and administration at the London School of Economics with continuing work in their main faculty and college. The scheme has proved attractive and is working well. Graduate students inform me that they have profited by a somewhat similar provision in the University of Toronto.

It is the other branch of the second stream of university students who present the main problem: those who pursue a particular academic course of study for its own sake, and who find more than enough in it to fire their imagination, discipline their minds, and maintain and develop their intellectual vigour and interest. The field of learning may be classics, philosophy, history, philology, a natural science, mathematics, archaeology, or what you will. The university honours graduate has a wider choice of careers open to him, and more understanding of their relative attractions, than the school-leaver, and as likely as not he will begin by being a little fastidious. The timeless quest for truth which, despite the looming spectre of the final examinations, the English university system aims to encourage during the middle period of a first degree course, is a world of intellectual paradise which, once enjoyed, a good scholar may be reluctant to abandon. The mundane discipline of the business life, the constant eye on the clock which efficient team work demands, do not always offer an immediately attractive prospect to the most highly trained intellects. Yet these are the type of leader that modern business needs, and the problems are how to attract them, and how to arrange the transition to the best advantage for both sides.

When this type of graduate considers the sort of life that business has to offer him, he may still be green enough in worldly experience to imagine that academic honours entitle him to privileged treatment, and the first test will come when he is disillusioned; but he will at least need to be assured that what his education has done to his mind will not have been done in vain. He will need, and expect, proper and efficient training, including the opportunity to learn fairly quickly what the firm does, how it does it, and why it is organized as it is. He will be impatient to know what new things he will need to study, in order to make the most of his opportunity and his training, and he will expect to be given reasonable assistance in going about that study. In short, he will assume that his employers will show an interest in his development and in capturing his interest and loyalty. He must not be allowed to develop a sense of frustration.

A really large concern will have the resources to organize its training with these aims in view, and the top-level positions of great responsibility in which vacancies have to be filled will usually offer a sufficient bait to attract the most ambitious beginner. It will need to offer nothing more than a full opportunity for advancement; and a declared policy of ruthlessly weeding out recruits who, given full opportunity, fail to merit retention and advancement will strengthen the appeal to the really good men, rather than deter them.

On the other hand, many of the best university graduates, whose studies do not happen to have ranged over the fields of economics, the organization of industry, and the specialization of business activity, will rightly hesitate to commit themselves to a business career, or to one type of enterprise rather than another, until they know more about the kind of life businessmen enjoy, the kind of issues and problems which have to be resolved, and the various alternatives offered by different kinds of business. Moreover, the sudden transition from student life to the status of an employee in a firm can be somewhat overwhelming in prospect. Even the good man who has decided to try his luck in business may well prefer to undergo some preliminary special study and training before attaching himself to, and beginning to show his paces in, the trainee group of a particular firm. A transitional university graduate course, designed to present to trained minds a balanced introduction to the various facets of business administration and to tune them up for their new field of activity, can prepare their digestions for the better assimilation of the practical training and experience which follow. The student will join the concern of his choice with greater confidence in the soundness of his decision, and with a clearer understanding of the place which the concern occupies in the general economy.

That, I imagine, is one aspect of the strength of the case for the graduate schools of business in the universities of the United States of America. It was certainly one of the prime purposes for establishing a generation ago at the London School of Economics in the University of London the graduate course in Business Administration, which extends over one academic year of full-time study, or two years if undertaken as part of the course for a M.Sc.Econ. degree in the special field of business administration. Because the seminar method of discussion, under the chairmanship of senior specialist professors and readers, is mainly employed, with full and continuous organized contribution by the students, the number admitted each year is limited to about twenty-five. In selecting the students, a balance is maintained of scientists, engineers, lawyers, and graduates in the humanities, and of graduates from the United Kingdom, the Commonwealth, Western Europe, the United States, and other parts of the world. Punctuality and regularity of attendance are insisted upon at all meetings. Not all professors conduct their seminars on identical lines; but in a typical case members of the course are trained to come prepared, to define at the outset the eternal questions which have to be given a quick provisional answer, to concentrate their attention on the matters which are relevant to the specific problem under discussion and for the elucidation of which the data have been brought to hand, and to reach their conclusions, subject to the comment and criticism of the instructor, before the seminar breaks up. By the time the course has ended, the participants have gained a fair idea of how business has to be conducted in most of the main types of commercial, financial, and industrial concerns. So far as the United Kingdom is concerned, very few of them have difficulty in finding the type of business opening they prefer, and all reports suggest that the same is true of those who come from and return to other parts of the world.

University courses of this character have other advantages. Because of their breadth of scope, they are complementary to the training schemes conducted within even the largest concerns, enabling the firms to concentrate more upon their own special needs. A large team of specialized teachers, experienced in the conduct of seminars, cannot really be assembled and maintained, with full academic freedom and opportunity for individual research, except in the conditions of detachment from special interests which universities and similar institutions provide. For the medium-sized and smaller concerns, which cannot afford to maintain training facilities continuously and with adequate strength, these university graduate courses are a special boon. They supply recruits to meet sporadic requirements, and the recruits come more widely trained than these concerns could arrange for from their own facilities.

What are the defects in the arrangement? The chief objection raised is that a graduate course of this character should be preceded by a period of practical experience. The suggestion has indeed been made that business concerns should organize their management-trainee schemes to extend over three years, the first to be devoted to giving the new graduate an over-all view of the activities of the business, the second to be spent in the university graduate school, and the third in further specialist training in the business in the field which the concern and the trainee agree is the most appropriate for his subsequent first period of responsible employment. The idea is excellent, and no university which maintains a graduate course would do other than welcome students who entered on such a basis. So far, however, it has not materialized. The difficulty is partly financial: the concern would have to pay the cost of maintaining the student attending the university course, with no guarantee that he would subsequently stay with them. Moreover, in conditions of full employment, concerns are short of staff, and do not look with favour on more prolonged periods of preliminary training. The best is the enemy of the good, and in prevailing conditions firms are so anxious to secure as many good men as they can that they are prepared to dispense with preliminary training altogether, and offer attractive starting salaries to new graduates. In special cases where the financial difficulty has been overcome by other means, the idea of preceding the year's attendance at a graduate course by a year's practical training has worked well. A good example is the Athlone Fellowship scheme under which Canadian engineering graduates spend two years in the United Kingdom. A number of these graduates have devoted the first year of their Fellowship to a course of training in an English factory and have followed it by full-time attendance in the graduate course in Business Administration at the London School of Economics. Several Toronto engineers have chosen to do this in recent years, and have then returned to Canada to enter manufacturing concerns.

Another objection to the timing of graduate courses is that they would be far more beneficial if the conditions of admission required *several years* of approved practical experience subsequent to graduation, so that the course could be designed to meet the needs of business executives with a background of really responsible administrative experience. Once again this is an excellent theory, but it rarely becomes practice and is unlikely to do so quickly on a significant scale. Not many concerns are likely to be prepared to second a really valuable executive for as long a period as a year, nor will the average executive respond eagerly to a suggestion that he should absent himself for so long, for fear of finding on his return that the concern has managed successfully without him and is somewhat embarrassed by the problem of arranging for his immediate reinstatement on terms satisfactory to both parties. Shorter courses are limited in scope and character in order to serve very different purposes.

A final criticism of graduate courses of the type I have described is their small output. If they are to maintain the quality of their service, the students are inevitably limited in each course to the number who can be brought individually and continuously into personal contact with senior specialist teachers in group discussions. By the adoption of other methods of teaching, involving mass lecture courses by the professors, supplemented by small-group tuition by numbers of junior instructors, far larger numbers could be accommodated, but the results would not be the same. These graduate courses depend for their success on teachers with a rare combination of knowledge, experience, and specialist teaching ability. In London the fact that the course is conducted in the London School of Economics, by teachers drawn from many large specialist departments of the social sciences, is mainly responsible for the success it has had, but nevertheless the expansion of its scale of operation is prevented by the lack of staff. Similar courses elsewhere will also continue to be confined to large university centres which can attract and afford the many specialists required.

The universities are under pressure to shorten their courses, and in particular to offer short vacation schools for the employees of firms seconded for the purpose. Such arrangements can clearly meet various needs: a weekend, a full week, a month can all be put to profitable use, but the provision of a graduate course conceived on the lines of that offered in London is not one of them. It is to be hoped that the pressure to attempt to do so will be resisted. If short-cuts of that kind could produce the same results, these obvious expedients would have been adopted long ago. And there is a further important consideration, the force of which is not so generally appreciated. University teachers have other uses to which to put their vacations. They need themselves to concentrate on the five R's, rehabilitation, reflection, research, relaxation, and, if time and strength permit, a little recreation.

Education for Business

Stanley F. Teele
John F. Chapman

The wave of economic and social change that has swept the United States and much of the world since World War II has already made it clear that the practice of management, if it is to be effectively carried on in the years ahead of us, is bound to undergo profound alteration. The explosive growth of population with its dramatic repercussions on our way of living, the breathtaking speed and scope of technological change, and now the inevitable swing to automation with all of its complex requirements for precise, long-range planning: these demand of tomorrow's executive a different type of background and skills than those to which we are accustomed. But what kind of background? And what skills? Who is prepared now to write the job description for the president of a steel mill in 1975? Or for the marketing director of a shoe factory? What will he need to know? What will he need to be able to do? What new concepts must he have in order to grasp the vastly enlarged scope of his business?

No one, either in the academic or in the business world, has precise answers to these questions yet, but the acute awareness of the problem in recent years is responsible for the feverish attention paid to the subject. Frederick Lewis Allen, writing in *Life* in 1953, stated neatly the complicated nature of the new executive requirements which need urgently to be recognized:

> The corporation executive today must be the captain of a smooth-working team of people who can decide whether the time has come to build a new polymerization plant, what the answer is to the unsatisfactory employee relations in a given unit of the business, how to cope with a new government regulation, how to achieve a mutually respectful understanding with union representatives and what position to take on price increases in order to maintain the good-will of the public. In short, he is confronted with so many questions which require knowledge, intellectual subtlety, political insight and human flexibility that he desperately needs a mental equipment of the sort that the old-time tycoon could do without.

The challenge posed by Mr. Allen has already been acknowledged by both the business and the academic worlds.

Throughout the business community, there is widespread recognition that tomorrow's executive must be able to move surely from policy to action in situations that will be different from anything any generation has experienced before. He must be able in quick succession to reach sound decisions relating to a new scientific development, a problem in government relations, and a new pricing programme. He must be able, as Crawford H. Greenewalt, president of du Pont, has observed, "to create a harmonious whole out of what the academic world calls dissimilar disciplines."

Other industrial leaders have spelled out in more detail what Mr. Greenewalt only hinted at. Perhaps the best statement of all these opinions is provided by Gilbert W. Chapman, president of the Yale & Towne Manufacturing Company and one of the most thoughtful analysts of the problem of our future managers. In a recent talk to Goddard College students, he declared:

> To meet the challenge of industry's new responsibility in the world of today requires a cultivation of mind and outlook that must come from the educational institutions of our land. My undergraduate days were spent in a school of engineering. After four years of this highly specialized training, I immediately began my business career in an American corporation. Since that time, it has become increasingly apparent to me that the problems of an executive become less specialized and more general or basic as the man advances toward the top. The specialist cannot function effectively at the top level of management if all he brings to it is his specialty. At that level, the daily problems call for broad general knowledge, open-mindedness, an understanding of human nature, an insight into human frailties, a fairness of mind, a clarity of thought—all these beyond the ordinary knowledge of a complex business problem. There must be an intellectual cultivation through which an individual views the main current of the life around him.

And then Mr. Chapman makes an important observation, one that is as significant to the academic world as it is to managers.

> The specialist is not excluded from a career in top management; it would be a little ridiculous for an engineer to suggest that. My contention is that the specialty alone, which thrives so well in the laboratory or research center, is in itself not sufficient qualification for top executive responsibility. Let the specialist extend his knowledge into the broader fields of general learning; then he, too, can move ahead—perhaps even more rapidly than others.

Leaders of thought in the field of business administration have developed some provocative observations concerning basic educational patterns for the business schools of the future. Looking ahead, they foresee that the number of facts—the body of knowledge—available to be learned by the business manager or prospective business manager seems likely to multiply tremendously. People who keep even moderately abreast of current business books and magazines cannot but be impressed by the proliferation of knowledge; indeed everyone in the field of university education for business is hard at work trying to add to this knowledge. The development of new mathematical and statistical theories and techniques, social science insights applicable to business, operations research, and long-range planning are all opening up whole new areas of importance to executives.

To such new areas as these, a manager must add the technical, economic, and social and political factors peculiar to his industry. On top of this is the specific information needed in a man's own company. Most university schools of business have pretty clearly and completely ruled out this last area of knowledge. Very few schools, if any, try to equip their graduates with knowledge at the individual company level. Many, moreover, have concluded that it is not possible to provide their graduates with much knowledge about particular industries. To this point, of course, there are notable exceptions. A good many schools, for instance, will provide a student with an immense amount of knowledge in concentrated courses about a particular subject such as insurance or real estate. Some direct their graduates to certain industries, such as petroleum, or are so located as to have the market for their graduates limited to only two or three industries.

Most schools, however, have focused on knowledge useful to the business administrator in such functions as accounting, marketing, and the like. The question then becomes: Is this *now* the proper emphasis? And with a steady, rapid increase in the available knowledge, will it be the proper emphasis *in the future*? The question deserves careful thought because it is one which plagues all professional education and indeed all education.

A number of round table discussions have been held recently with representative leaders in education for medicine, law, engineering, and so on. The most striking features of these conferences have been the extent to which representatives of each profession were expressing the same basic ideas, each in his way. In effect the medical people were saying: 'The body of medical knowledge is now so great that we can't possibly hope to teach it to a man; instead, we should try to teach a man to think like a doctor.' The lawyers were saying: 'The body of knowledge about the law is now so great that we can't possibly teach it to a man; the most we can do is to teach him to think like a lawyer.' Even the engineers have moved in this direction.

The thinking at the Harvard Business School has been along the same lines, and the School has been working to give form to these ideas for a good many years. As a result of the experience acquired to date, the administration at the School believes that both a knowledge of facts and wisdom—or the capacity for judging soundly and dealing broadly with facts—are important for the business manager, but that wisdom is vastly the more important of the two. Furthermore, the Harvard Business School has arrived at the conviction that knowledge—facts about a specific industry or a specific company—can most effectively be acquired in the later years. At Harvard the major educational emphasis has been on finding ways to help men develop the capacity of judging soundly and dealing broadly with facts, rather than on the teaching of the facts themselves. Whatever success the School has had over the years derives more from this continuing attempt than from any other.

Clarence Randall, in his recent lectures at Harvard, epitomized what educators in the field of business administration are coming to recognize as basic in planning for the future:

> I fear that as a nation we Americans are in danger of yielding to technical hypnosis. We behave at times as though we believe that all problems can be resolved by the process of physical research and the application of engineering methods. The lesson of my own business experience is that this is not so, and that the art of management, even in an industry that rests for its success on the achievements of the scientist and engineer requires a broadly cultivated mind.

Because the Harvard Business School has long been concerned with the problem of a sound liberal education for prospective managers, the *Harvard Business Review* has carried several articles relating to the subject. In one of the most popular, Frederic E. Pamp, Jr., writing on "Liberal Arts as Training for Business," summarizes the direct applicability of the liberal arts and social sciences to the *process of decision* of the manager by demonstrating that three kinds of disciplines prepare people directly for the skills and qualities needed by the administrator:

> 1. The executive must distinguish and define the possible lines of action among which a choice can be made. This requires imagination, the ability to catch at ideas, shape them into concrete form, and present them in terms appropriate to the problem.
> 2. He must analyse the consequences of taking each line of action. Here the computer and operations research techniques can do much, but the

executive must set the framework for the problems from his experience and his imagination, and work with his own sensitivity and knowledge in the area of human beings where statistics and scientific prediction are highly fallible guides.

3. Then in the decision he must have the grasp to know its implications in all areas of an organism which is itself far from being absolutely predictable; the company, the market, the economy, and the society.

Important strides have been made by both industry and business to meet this need for a new type of manager.

Universities in the United States have offered special programmes in the field of Business Administration ever since the Wharton School of Finance and Commerce was founded in 1881 as an undergraduate school at the University of Pennsylvania, but the number of such schools remained small up to World War II, and no standard pattern dominated them.

Harvard's Graduate School of Business Administration, now the country's largest, was founded in 1908, and has from the first been a graduate school offering a two-year programme leading to the degree of Master of Business Administration. In contrast, the Amos Tuck School at Dartmouth, which also grants a Master of Business Administration degree, is based on a five-year combination undergraduate and graduate programme, the first two years of which are devoted to liberal arts. The bulk of the courses in business administration are taught in the last three years. Currently there are 74 schools in the American Association of Collegiate Schools of Business, the central accrediting organization for the whole country of all schools offering degrees in Business Administration at either the undergraduate or graduate level.

The educational programme which seems to come closest to preparing the ideal executives for the future, at least according to the standards now emerging, is apparently one which provides an undergraduate degree in liberal arts or engineering, and a graduate course in business administration in one of the schools featuring the rounded background demanded by such men as Gilbert Chapman and Frederic Pamp. Actually, the number of graduates from such courses in the United States now is small. The Harvard Business School, with the largest single group, graduates about 600 men each year.

Undergraduate training of the men in these courses varies. At Harvard, approximately one quarter of most entering classes since World War II hold an engineering degree. Of the liberal arts graduates, about 20 per cent have majored in business administration, 25 per cent in the social sciences, 16 per cent in the humanities, and 3 per cent in government.

All of the major schools are attempting to meet the demand for broader gauge executives in the future by stressing problems of labour relations and human relations, and by offering courses in administrative practices which stress the human factor in management. At Harvard, one of the most popular courses is Business Responsibilities in the American Society, where problems of government and community relations are explored, and where basic ethical values are considered as a part of the decision-making process.

Another way in which students are trained for group action in several of the graduate schools where the case method of teaching is used and report writing is an integral part of the programme, is to train the students in groups. Harvard deliberately organizes the students into fairly large classes so that there can be a wide diversity of points of view brought to bear on each case that is studied. But to provide a maximum of discussion, classes are divided into study groups of eight or ten to explore in advance all aspects of the problem presented in the case. After this first distillation, handled informally by the smaller student groups, the class can quickly dig into the basic points as each group has lined them up in its preliminary discussion. In this way, potential executives are taught to work as a team in exploring a situation with each man making a contribution for the group to weigh. Similarly, when the time comes for field research on a specific problem, groups of students undertake the assignment, and the final report is a joint effort on which the grade of each member of the group is determined.

While this programme, with four years of undergraduate work in engineering or liberal arts followed by two years of specialization in business administration, seems to come closest to providing the ideal candidate for tomorrow's management positions, not all students are able to afford the cost or spend the six years that are required to complete the programme. For this group, two basic types of four-year programmes are offered—both approved by the A.A.C.S.B.

The first calls for two years of regular liberal arts courses at the beginning of the college programme, followed by two years of specialized training in business administration. The University of Kansas is typical of the Schools which have developed this kind of programme. Advocates claim that the main advantage of this system is the opportunity it provides for students to mature in the first two formative years out of high school and to be exposed to the subjects which are believed to be most effective in training people to do original thinking. With this foundation they are expected to grapple more effectively with the business subjects in their last two years.

The Wharton School, on the other hand, has worked during the entire seventy-five years of its existence on the premise that a business programme is most effective when spread over the entire four years, with liberal arts subjects included each year.

There is no agreement at the moment among educational leaders as to which system is preferable, and as long as a minimum number of business courses are included, there is likely to be no attempt to alter local patterns. It is significant, however, that among 74 schools which are members of the A.A.C.S.B., 40 per cent of the subject-hours taught are in non-business subjects. While leaders in the group are inclined to stress the need for more intensive teaching of English, and possibly of the social sciences, there is no tendency yet to demand more hours of work in either field.

It is in the liberal arts colleges, however, that one of the most striking developments is taking place. Confronted with the local demand that has persisted now for more than thirty years to provide courses in business administration, some so-called liberal arts colleges are actually offering a wider variety of subjects in the field than the business schools offer. A part of this demand has come from local industry which has sought the aid of local schools in interesting students in their field. Fourteen universities in the United States, for example, offer courses in ceramics.

What is ahead for the liberal arts college in the face of the soaring demand for people trained in business and, at the same time, the demand from scores of successful executives that more attention be devoted to the humanities as a sound foundation for executive training? The fact that industry itself is turning to the colleges for help in broadening the background of its executives at the middle and advanced management levels may well revive the popularity of courses in literature, history, the arts, and mathematics. Certainly, several recent moves by industry have revived the prestige of classical professors at a number of Eastern colleges.

This unusual precedent was established as long ago as 1953 by the Bell system when it set up a ten-month Institute of Humanistic Studies, to be conducted by the University of Pennsylvania. Executives of the system devoted the entire year to the study of literature, art, history, languages, or any subject of their choice, and the experiment was sufficiently successful for Bell later to authorize eight-week summer courses at Dartmouth and Williams Colleges, each with 40 men enrolled, and one of 14 weeks at Swarthmore when 20 managers from 14 companies in the Bell system participated.

It is significant, however, that there has been no all-out swing—by Bell or by other companies with vigorous executive training programmes —to this highly specialized form of liberalizing and broadening the backgrounds of specialists among their managers. While more special courses of this kind may be offered for men who failed to receive a truly liberal education during their college years, the major trend is to provide prospective managers in their training for business with the kind of interchange of thought between faculty and student, or even student and student, which rounds their background at the same time that it teaches them to think. For this purpose the case method is being widely used throughout industry in its management training programmes. Properly applied, it provides the stimulation and the interchange which seems to do most to create broad and logical thinking among the trainees.

Educators, seeking to find the ideal programme of education to provide business with men of the calibre to take over management roles in the complex economy in which we must operate in the future, plot a three-part programme:

1. Four years of undergraduate study in a liberal arts programme in which heavy emphasis is placed on English, mathematics, the natural sciences, history, and philosophy or psychology. Ideal objectives of this period in a prospective manager's education might be:

(a) To develop an understanding of the social, political, and economic changes—both national and international—which will influence the problems of corporate management to an increasingly greater degree in the future. This might be defined as developing a breadth of outlook, looking towards future "statesmanship" in business.

(b) To indicate the importance, impact, and use of history, science, philosophy, and the arts in the world today, particularly as they influence large groups of people, such as employees, customers, and stockholders.

(c) To motivate the participants in the programme to accept the concept that intellectual activity is a never-ending process to be continued throughout their lives.

(d) To balance with a humanistic background the almost complete attention generally given by younger men to the acquiring of technical knowledge and competence as a result of working in an atmosphere of intense competition with other individuals.

(*e*) To offset a tendency to over-conformity, which is bound to occur in a business which is highly specialized and which promotes almost entirely from within the organization.

In addition to this mind-stretching experience, today's educators recommend a planned series of summer vacations. These might include travel, an experiment in living with a family in a foreign country, or work in specific fields which would help to focus the interests of the student. The objective, as in the case of the college courses themselves, is to broaden the horizons of the individual and make him increasingly aware of the wonders and the problems in the world around him.

2. Two to four years of business experience following graduation from college. Educators attach special significance to this period during which the student attempts to apply what he has learned to the specific problems of business, and to gain a realistic insight into the way the economy works.

3. A two-year programme in a graduate school of business administration. Here the emphasis would be almost entirely on the development of the skills of an administrator. Equipped with a sound basic education and matured by two or more years in business, the student should be ready to get the most out of a programme which has been designed to focus all his background and experience onto the solution of problems as they have developed in actual business situations.

Even as they make these recommendations, educators know that they represent an ideal which few students can afford, and many do not yet seek. What encourages them to think in this direction, however, is the increasing tendency of management in the most progressive companies to plan and finance advanced training for promising men in the middle management group, or in the advanced group, who need all the skills they can command to cope with the problems of the next ten to twenty years. If men at these ages are going to come back to professional business schools after five to twenty years on the job, then it becomes increasingly important that they come with the broadest possible educational backgrounds. Otherwise, they may lack the breadth of interest and mental flexibility to permit them to profit from belated specialized training in making decisions.

*

While the preparation of men for business administration is by all odds the greatest single relationship between the universities and business, there are other ways in which the two co-operate.

From the time the Harvard Business School was founded it has aggressively sought out businesses with unsolved administrative problems. Some of these have been incorporated into cases as the basis for classroom discussion, which the managers of the company involved can attend. In other situations, the Business School's Division of Research has undertaken major studies of administrative problems, with interested companies sometimes helping to defray costs. But the largest field of research is that initiated by the faculty or the School in areas where management may know that a problem is developing but has not been able to detach itself from the day-to-day operations long enough to pinpoint it and initiate research to solve it. It is in this broad area that the business schools are making some of their most valuable contributions to business. At the present time, 46 research projects are under way at Harvard, and approximately 50 present or past members of the senior faculty are actively participating in them. The projects range from a study of "Management and Automation," "A Case of Organizational Change," and "Managing Decentralized Companies," to a five-year study of the "Effectiveness of Executive Development Programmes," and a long-range study on "Consumer Motivation Research and Related Management Problems."

Through these studies and the research that goes into them the Harvard Business School faculty maintains a close contact with industry and its day-to-day problems, and provides inquiring managements with suggestions about the ways in which some of their most pressing problems can be solved. In addition, faculty members in most schools of business are encouraged to undertake a limited number of consulting assignments with industries which are aggressively tackling basic business problems. In this way, industry benefits from some of the best independent thinking and research that is being done at the theoretical level, and faculty members maintain contact with managements and the new problems that arise every week.

Business schools also work with major foundations on problems which are basic to all industries. One such project currently under way at Harvard is the conducting of a summer seminar for deans of business schools and professors of business administration. Financed by the Ford Foundation, the summer seminars are designed to help meet the pressing demands for more and better teachers of business administration by sharing with them in concentrated form the experience which Harvard has developed in fifty years of teaching by the case method.

Even before this project developed, the Harvard Business School had stepped up its programme of teacher development in anticipation of the demand that the great bulge in the national birth-rate in the last fifteen years will soon bring increased college enrolments. The children who will be of college age in the 1960's are already inundating the elementary and secondary schools, and, while no one knows how many will actually attend college, estimates range from a 100 to a 400 per cent increase above present totals. Either prediction poses acute problems.

The doctoral programme at the Harvard Business School has for some time been an important link between the need and the fulfilment of the demand for well-qualified teachers of business administration. As long as five years ago the Business School, foreseeing the growing need for teachers of business administration, initiated a committee study of its doctoral programme and, following receipt of the results of this study, revamped the entire programme and planned its enlargement.

From a rate of three doctoral degrees a year during the first twenty-five years of the programme, the tempo has now been stepped up to twenty a year. Emphasis has been placed on attracting more men who have done graduate work elsewhere, and who want now to concentrate on the teaching system in the field of business education as it has developed at Harvard.

The new programme, besides offering doctoral candidates more intensive and special training under the direct guidance of five or six faculty members who handle this project as their principal assignment, provides specific training in research methods appropriate to research in business administration, and a seminar in teaching by the case method. Thus, in this revamping of its programme, the Harvard Business School has both refined its training techniques for prospective teachers of business administration and increased its capacity to help meet the critical needs for teachers in the years ahead.

In its effort to meet the new conditions which currently confront business leaders, Harvard has pioneered in new areas which it feels may have an important bearing on business education in the future. One such project, now entering its second year, is the summer seminar on "Religion and Ethics in Business Policy Decisions." Sponsored by the Danforth Foundation, the seminar is designed to meet constructively the growing awareness among many executives that the deepest religious and ethical, as well as technical, insights are required of them and the increasing realization by teachers of the role that religious and ethical values should play in their responsibilities both in and outside the classroom.

Harvard, like some other business schools, has also developed close working relations with a group of industries known as Associates. These industries contribute annually to the continuing research projects at the Business School, pose problems on which they seek help, and share ahead of general release in all of the findings of the Division of Research. Through the Associates, members of the faculty are able to carry out many of their on-the-spot surveys and analyses, and through the School the Associates acquire a management research arm to supplement their own internal organization.

Finally, to share with the whole business community the best of current thinking on administrative problems, the School publishes the *Harvard Business Review*. Though designed originally to bring to a far larger audience than the student body the results of all research conducted at the Business School, the publication long ago opened its pages to outstanding research reports from other schools and from industry, and over the thirty-five years since it was established has helped to provide a bridge between the academic world and the world of business.

What the world of business needs in order to meet tomorrow's challenge is a steady stream of creative men with a broad knowledge and a capacity for independent thinking. This calls for men who will pursue ideas, who will seek to solve problems, although they may have nothing to do with the immediate problems before them—men whose thinking does not end with the business day and who, through their education, have learned that one of the greatest joys in life is to be able to think for one's self.

The United States can produce through its schools men of the calibre and vision to meet tomorrow's challenge to management, but it will produce them in sufficient quantity and with sufficient speed only if the business and the academic worlds see the problem clearly and join forces to solve it.

Lightning Source UK Ltd.
Milton Keynes UK
UKHW012358200722
406167UK00001B/304